Pádraig Ó Fathaigh's War of Independence

Recollections of a Galway Gaelic Leaguer

IRISH NARRATIVES

IRISH NARRATIVES

Series edited by David Fitzpatrick

Personal narratives of past lives are essential for understanding any field of history. They provide unrivalled insight into the day-to-day consequences of political, social, economic or cultural relationships. Memoirs, diaries and personal letters, whether by public figures or obscure witnesses of historical events, will often captivate the general reader as well as engrossing the specialist. Yet the vast majority of such narratives are preserved only among the manuscripts or rarities in libraries and archives scattered over the globe. The aim of this series of brief yet scholarly editions is to make available a wide range of narratives concerning Ireland and the Irish over the last four centuries. All documents, or sets of documents, are edited and introduced by specialist scholars, who guide the reader through the world in which the text was created. The chosen texts are faithfully transcribed, the biographical and local background explored, and the documents set in historical context. This series will prove invaluable for university and school teachers, providing superb material for essays and textual analysis in class. Above all, it offers a novel opportunity for readers interested in Irish history to discover fresh and exciting sources of personal testimony.

Other titles in the series:

Andrew Bryson's Ordeal: An Epilogue to the 1798 Rebellion, edited by Michael Durey

Henry Stratford Persse's Letters from Galway to America, 1821–1832, edited by James L. Pethica and James C. Roy

A Redemptorist Missionary in Ireland, 1851–1854: Memoirs by Joseph Prost, C.Ss.R. translated and edited by Emmet Larkin and Herman Freudenberger

Frank Henderson's Easter Rising: Recollections of a Dublin Volunteer, edited by Michael Hopkinson

A Patriot Priest: The Life of Father James Coigly, 1761–1798, edited by Dáire Keogh

'My Darling Danny': Letters from Mary O'Connell to Her Son Daniel, 1830–1832, edited by Erin I. Bishop

The Rebel in his Family: Selected Papers of William Smith O'Brien, edited by Richard and Marianne Davis

The Reynolds Letters: An Irish Emigrant Family in Late Victorian Manchester, edited by Lawrence W. McBride

A Policeman's Ireland: Recollections of Samuel Waters, RIC, edited by Stephen Ball

'The Misfit Soldier': Edward Casey's War Story, 1914–1918, edited by Joanna Bourke

Alfred Webb: The Autobiography of a Quaker Nationalist, edited by Marie-Louise Legg

Forthcoming titles:

'As I was among the Captives': Joseph Campbell's Prison Diary, 1922–1923, edited by Eiléan Ní Chuilleanáin

An Englishwoman in Belfast: Rosamond Stephen's Record of the Great War, edited by Oonagh Walsh

David Fitzpatrick teaches history at Trinity College, Dublin. His books include *Politics and Irish Life, 1913–1921* (1977, reissued 1998), *Oceans of Consolation: Personal Accounts of Irish Migration to Australia* (1995) and *The Two Irelands, 1912–1939* (1998).

Pádraig Ó Fathaigh's War of Independence

Recollections of a Galway Gaelic Leaguer

Edited by
Timothy G. McMahon

Cork University Press

First published in 2000 by
Cork University Press
Cork
Ireland

British Library Cataloguing in Publication Data
A CIP catalogue record for this book is available from the British Library.
ISBN 1 85918 145 7

Typesetting by Red Barn Publishing, Skeagh, Skibbereen

Printed and bound by CPI Antony Rowe, Eastbourne

Reprinted 2007 2007

Contents

Acknowledgements

The editor wishes to acknowledge the assistance and kind permission of the Ó Fathaigh family to publish this work and the cover photograph. In particular, I wish to thank Finian in Galway city and Sr Íde in the Convent of Mercy, Elphin, County Roscommon, for providing me with so much additional information about Pádraig Ó Fathaigh, his work and his family. This book would not have been possible without their help. I should also like to thank the kind people from south Galway who offered materials — including photographs — for my use, but which unfortunately could not be used in the present volume. Specifically, I must thank Thomas Quinn of Crushoa, Kinvara; Michael Loughrey of Scarriff, Tubber; and the Beagh Rural Development Association. I owe a significant debt of gratitude to Peadar Mac Fhlannchadha of Conradh na Gaeilge, Gaillimh, who not only provided information but helped to put me in touch with the Ó Fathaigh family. I also wish to thank the staff in the Manuscripts Department at the National Library of Ireland and the Council of Trustees of the NLI for their permission to publish from the Ó Fathaigh Papers. For their patience and guidance, I should also like to thank my general editor, Professor David Fitzpatrick, and Sara Wilbourne and the Cork University Press. Special thanks also go out to Professor James S. Donnelly, Jr, of the University of Wisconsin–Madison; Matthew O'Brien and Michael DeNie, also at Madison, for their suggestions; Breandán Mac Suibhne for first telling me about *Irish Narratives*; Stephen Ball for advice about the RIC and for tracing Constable Patrick Durkan; and Fergus Campbell for general discussions about politics in County Galway at the turn of the century. Any misstatements or omissions are, of course, my responsibility. My greatest debts, as always, are to Liam and Anne.

Introduction

'Is Éireannach mé' — 'I am an Irishman.' Written in response to a police interrogator in 1919, this simple declaration encapsulates the defiant mindset which led Pádraig Ó Fathaigh (1879–1976) to fight for Irish freedom between 1916 and 1921. In 1968 Ó Fathaigh outlined his part in this struggle in two overlapping memoirs, one handwritten in English and the other an Irish-language typescript. Both are currently held along with some related papers in the National Library of Ireland in Dublin. What follows comes from the English-language account, which is the more complete in its details of Ó Fathaigh's political activities during the Irish War of Independence. In the eight years between 1914 and 1922 he met almost every major figure in the Irish republican movement, yet his own field of operation was largely confined to within fifty miles of his birthplace at Lurgan, Gort, County Galway. Thus, with its focus on one man's experiences of incarceration and guerrilla warfare, this memoir reveals the energetic and self-effacing Ó Fathaigh as a representative of those who all too often disappear from the pages of history — the local activists who shape the way that national movements take root among the common people.

Ó Fathaigh's account is reminiscent of other records of the same period, such as Colm Ó Gaora's *Mise* or Michael Brennan's *The War in Clare*; however, this work offers unique insights into prison life and life on the run during the 'Troubles'. In particular, we learn about the men who had been court-martialled for their actions during the Easter Rising, many of whom played leading roles in the foundation of the Irish state. On a later occasion Ó Fathaigh participated in the hunger-strike at London's Wormwood Scrubs prison in 1920. At the time it was a pivotal incident, but it has since been overshadowed by its more famous contemporaries — the hunger-strikes at Dundalk, Belfast and Mountjoy prisons. Ó Fathaigh also served as an Intelligence Officer in the IRA's Gort Brigade and as adjutant in an active service unit of the Mid-Clare Brigade. Through these recollections, he captures the experience of Ireland's provincial guerrilla war: the drudgery of waiting for ambushes which do not materialise; the narrow escapes from capture; the sudden eruptions of violence inherent in a conflict waged literally alongside everyday civilian life.

Thematically, the memoir divides into three sections: the first deals with Ó Fathaigh's four stints in jail between 1916 and 1920; the second begins in the late summer of 1920 and follows him during the guerrilla campaign waged in Counties Galway and Clare; the third discusses the political and military reorganisation in County Galway from the truce between British and republican forces in July 1921 until the so-called 'Pact Election' of 1922. Although the final segment follows the other two in both structural and chronological progression, readers may find that certain of its passages help to clarify events referred to in earlier portions of the text. In particular, those sections dealing with 'Galway City' and 'Intelligence Officers' display Ó Fathaigh's appreciation of the political diversity in his home county and, by extension, in Ireland as a whole.

I

In 1914 the question of granting Home Rule to Ireland held centre stage in the United Kingdom. Since the Parliament Act of 1911 had restricted the veto power of the House of Lords, the potential existed for the Liberal government to fulfil its longstanding commitment to pass a Home Rule Bill. Parliament debated the issue, spurred on by the Liberals' dependence on support from the Irish Parliamentary Party led by the moderate nationalist John Redmond. Opponents of Home Rule — based mainly in Ulster — were increasingly well organised and vocal, and in September 1912 the Ulster Unionist Council had sponsored a 'Solemn League and Covenant' through which nearly a quarter of a million people pledged themselves to oppose Home Rule by 'all means which may be found necessary'. Their rhetoric took on an ominous, tangible form with the formation of the paramilitary Ulster Volunteer Force. In response — and, indeed, in tribute to the UVF — Eoin MacNeill and Pádraig Pearse called for the establishment of a similar 'national guard' to defend the rights of Irishmen to govern themselves. At a meeting in Dublin in November 1913 MacNeill took the lead in establishing the Irish Volunteers, composed mainly of southern Home Rulers, but also including, *sub rosa*, a substantial number of IRB men in key positions.[1]

If Home Rule was the Irish Parliamentary Party's major goal in 1914, its popular support had long been rooted in its commitment to overhauling landlord–tenant relations. Since 1879, when the Land War erupted in County Mayo, tenant farmers and landless labourers pressed for rent relief and the redistribution of farmland through a wide range of extraparliamentary intimidatory tactics — from arson to boycotting; from shooting at persons and property to withholding rents; from breaking down fences to driving cattle off ranches. Such acts augmented, and at times diverted, the work undertaken by Charles Stewart Parnell and his parliamentary successors for nearly two generations.

Born on Christmas Day 1879, as the fifth of six children, Pádraig Ó Fathaigh grew up in the shadow of these events. Farmers on estates and ranches near his home periodically engaged in agrarian agitations during the following thirty years.[2] Whether his parents, Laurence and Bridget, or any of his five siblings were involved in these campaigns is unclear, but they would not have been far removed from them. In the parishes around Gort tenant farmers like the Ó Fathaighs still relied on the communal farming techniques traditional in rural Ireland. Teams of men often worked together building homes on each other's farmsteads, and the common harvesting and threshing, known as the *meitheal*, remained customary during Pádraig's youth. As with most of their neighbours, the Ó Fathaighs lived in a three-roomed house and raised grains, root crops and livestock for sale at local markets. They also maintained a few outbuildings for their animals, indicating that the family was able to invest in some improvements on their farm.[3]

Like many of his contemporaries, Pádraig lived and worked at his parents' home as a 'farmer's son' well into his twenties; indeed, he resided at Lurgan, unmarried, until after the War of Independence.[4] But in the early years of the new century his love of the Irish language allowed him to take a crucial step towards personal independence through involvement in the Gaelic revival.

Since 1893 the Gaelic League had sought to preserve and extend the use of Irish as a spoken language. Through its language classes, concerts and festivals, the League encouraged people to think of Gaelic as both a symbol of Ireland's heritage and a badge of enduring cultural distinctiveness. Such sentiments resonated strongly with Ó Fathaigh, who took intense pride in the language his family still spoke in their home. He wrote poetry for competitions at League-sponsored festivals, and in 1907 one of his songs won a prize at the regional Feis Connacht, enabling him to attend the Gaelic summer college at Toormakeady, County Mayo. There he received his certification to teach Irish in National Schools. For the next two years he assisted the travelling teacher (*múinteoir taistil*) for the League's Gort district on a part-time basis; and in 1909 Pádraig himself became the district's full-time *múinteoir taistil*.[5]

The very nature of his duties necessitated that Ó Fathaigh be flexible, creative, and highly organised — qualities which were also crucial in his later political career. The district council expected him to teach Irish during the day in the National Schools and at night in League branches throughout south Galway. Each week he criss-crossed an area of more than a hundred square miles, riding his bicycle on wet, poorly maintained roads. His night classes grew to as large as 150 pupils, and because the students ranged in age and proficiency from young schoolchildren who were just learning Irish to adults in their seventies who had spoken it all their lives, Pádraig varied his lesson plans to broaden their appeal. Singing and dancing lessons augmented instruction in reading and coversation; students produced short plays in Irish, such as Douglas Hyde's *An Posadh* ('The Marriage'); and the Ardrahan and Castledaly branches sponsored their own *feiseanna*. Thus, in addition to developing extraordinary physical stamina through his travels, Pádraig became familiar with the countryside and friendly with many people in the district. All of which proved invaluable to him when he joined the Volunteers in 1914 and began recruiting from among his students.[6]

Whether Ó Fathaigh had also joined the Irish Republican Brotherhood by then remains unclear, though in all probability he had done so. Given his mobility and his family's apparent political sympathies, he would have been a likely candidate for recruitment. Other itinerant Gaelic League teachers and organisers — such as Colm Ó Gaora and Seán Ó Muirthile — joined the IRB between 1912 and 1914, suggesting that this may have been when Ó Fathaigh joined.[7] We can infer, moreover, from what he writes that his family held opinions which may indicate an earlier affiliation. The family subscribed to the *United Irishman*, a newspaper founded by Arthur Griffith in 1899, and they held on to their copies of the paper until the police confiscated them during the Troubles. Pádraig himself served as secretary of the local 1798 Centenary Committee — one of many loosely affiliated groups aligned with the IRB at the turn of the century. His older brothers, Míchéal and Seán, also joined the Volunteers, with Seán serving as adjutant of the Ballycahalan Company, and their youngest sister, Mary, became secretary of the local chapter of the republican women's organisation, Cumann na mBan. Indeed, the family home at Lurgan served as a favoured abode for Liam Mellows when he arrived in the region in 1915 to drill companies of Volunteers and recruit on behalf of the IRB.

County Galway at this time was a politically diverse community. Ó Fathaigh tells us in the latter pages of his memoir that both the city and county had a sizeable number of 'loyalists', some of whom were professionals or from the dwindling ranks of the landed elite, while others were connected to the military and police services. In the eyes of the more separatist-minded people in the county, Galway city had the reputation of being a 'garrison town'. One can also point to 'secret society' men and republicans who were active in Galway politics and land agitations before 1916, but they remained a minority in much of the county. In certain communities, such as Gurteen, the Irish Parliamentary Party's constituent organisation, the United Irish League, refused the aid of 'secret society' men on land questions. Even a phrase like 'the Irish Volunteers' is problematic. In September and October 1914 Volunteer companies throughout Ireland split over whether or not to support Britain in the Great War. Redmond, in an effort to shore up goodwill for Home Rule, encouraged them to assist the war effort, and the vast majority agreed with the party leader. Nevertheless, tensions developed between these 'National' Volunteers and the smaller corps of 'Irish' Volunteers who believed their fight was within Ireland. To cite just one example of the bitter division created at this time, a Redmondite company of National Volunteers was formed in Galway city on 18 October 1914. Just two nights earlier a large crowd had jeered and broken windows at the home of solicitor George Nicholls, a local Sinn Féin leader and chairman of the county's Irish Volunteers.[8]

Moreover, the police remained a significant presence in the county. The constabulary's distinguishing trait since the Land War was its intimate knowledge of the people, based on a combination of their performance of non-police functions and intelligence-gathering. By 1900 the composition of the force was fairly representative of the general population, consisting mainly of Catholic farmers' or farm labourers' sons. To prevent association with friends or relatives, the RIC insisted that its constables serve outside their home counties and on occasion to live in barracks apart from their wives and children. With a dearth of civil servants in the provinces, constables acted in their stead, collecting information on the harvests, issuing dog licences and enumerating the census. By definition, however, their most important duties involved peacekeeping and law enforcement. District inspectors and head constables watched for signs of agrarian unrest or republican activity on behalf of the RIC's Special Branch. In areas like south Galway, therefore, the popular memory associated the RIC with efforts to uphold eviction notices and to break up tenant combinations. It is little wonder that Ó Fathaigh, like other separatists, developed an obvious antipathy towards 'the eyes and ears of Dublin Castle', an antipathy encapsulated in Ó Fathaigh's Gaelic shorthand term for the police — 'shee weera' [*sidhe Mhuire*], a prying busybody.[9]

It is a testimony to Ó Fathaigh's ingenuity that there is no mention of him in the RIC's monthly reports until 1918 — particularly in view of his growing responsibilities in the Volunteer and IRB command structures. When the Volunteer split occurred in October 1914, he sided with those companies which rejected Redmond's call to fight in the Great War and became secretary of the Galway County Board of the Volunteers. He worked with Nicholls and Mellows, as well as with the brigade commandant, Laurence Lardner, who served on the IRB Supreme Council in 1917. Early in 1916 he accompanied Lardner and Mellows to a meeting in Limerick at which Pádraig Pearse informed IRB men from Counties Limerick, Clare and Galway about the IRB Military Council's plans for the rebellion at Easter.[10]

Ó Fathaigh's treatment of the rising — which began in County Galway on Tuesday 25 April — is understandably brief. Mellows had dispatched him to bring Father J. W. O'Meehan of Kinvara to serve as quartermaster for the main force of Volunteers, but police overpowered and arrested him at Kinvara presbytery, cutting him off from Mellows and Lardner at Athenry. In the best account of the western rising, Desmond Greaves suggests that Mellows attempted to free Ó Fathaigh when he learned of the latter's arrest. Mellows and his men anticipated that the police would move Pádraig to Galway city; instead they had taken him to Limerick. Thus, while Mellows's party encountered some resistance at Oranmore — the 'opening rounds' of Easter week in the west — there was no significant confrontation, and Ó Fathaigh remained in custody.[11]

Over the next two days more than 600 people joined Mellows and Lardner. Most were poorly armed and poorly trained, but, according to Greaves, their spirits were high because they encountered little initial resistance and because their actions, apparently, met with public approval. Unnerved by the revolt, the RIC hastily abandoned their more isolated barracks and concentrated their forces in larger towns to await reinforcement. This action left the Volunteers free to move about a 600-square-mile area of the county. In the districts surrounding Loughrea, Athenry, Gort, Tuam and Galway large numbers of people openly supported the rebels. Greaves records that farmers near Athenry sent their daughters to Mellows's camp with gifts of food and milk, and the RIC in the West Riding of the county believed that 'practically all' of the country people 'were in sympathy with the rebels at the time directly or indirectly'. According to the County Inspector, such a large percentage of the young men in these districts committed 'overt acts of rebellion' that only arrests, internments and courts martial 'restored order and brought matters back to their normal state'.[12]

By early May police and military forces throughout Ireland had rounded up more than 3,100 men and women, deporting 2,500 to Britain without trial. Beginning in early June, under the authority of the Defence of the Realm Act, the government held about 1,800 of them in Frongoch internment camp in Wales. Among these prisoners were 322 men from County Galway, a total second only to that from County Dublin.[13] By mid-August a special judicial advisory committee had reviewed most of their cases and had recommended that more than 1,100 be released. The rest remained at Frongoch until December 1916. Still another group of prisoners had faced formal courts martial in the aftermath of Easter week. Most famously, fourteen of their leaders were executed at Kilmainham Jail between 3 May and 12 May. Of the remaining 120 or so, most received extended sentences of penal servitude in England until they were freed by an amnesty on 17 June 1917. Ó Fathaigh was one of these men. The discipline, friendships and communications networks built up among the Irish prisoners during these months shaped developments during the Anglo-Irish War.

The execution of the rising's leaders and the imprisonment of thousands began to transform Irish nationalist opinion and to direct it against Britain and Redmond's party. Unwittingly the government ensured the manner in which this changing mindset manifested itself between 1916 and 1919 by focusing its 'mild coercion' on the reconstituted Volunteer companies and the emerging Sinn Féin party. Inexorably the administration's attentions escalated tensions with this aggressive nationalist phalanx. Police repeatedly arrested Volunteer and Sinn Féin leaders and searched their homes for seditious literature. Beginning in 1917, many of these men and women denied the authority of 'British' courts to judge their cases and of 'British' jails to hold them. When not behind bars, they sought to isolate the police from the public, cutting the RIC off from sources of information through persuasion and intimidation.[14] In July 1918 Dublin Castle declared organisations like Sinn Féin, the Volunteers, the Gaelic League and Cumann na mBan to be 'dangerous,' and the administration extended the wartime Defence of the Realm Regulations to require prior approval from the police before any group held a public meeting. Volunteer companies responded by drilling openly, and Sinn Féin branches courted baton charges by the police by holding unsanctioned gatherings.

Meanwhile, with the outcome of the war in Europe still uncertain, parliament passed a bill extending conscription to Ireland in April 1918. More than any other issue, the threatened application of conscription solidified growing anti-government feeling and swelled the ranks of Sinn Féin. In the midst of the anti-conscription campaign, the government arrested some seventy Sinn Féin leaders on the pretext that they were negotiating with the German Empire. This so-called 'German Plot' was prompted by the capture of Joseph Dowling — a former Irish prisoner-of-war — who had been placed off the coast of County Clare by a German submarine in April 1917. The arrests initially raised questions about the party's viability, but they eventually rallied more support to Sinn Féin and the Volunteers.[15]

In south Galway two other factors aided the party's growth. First, a large number of Catholic curates lent their support to the movement, presiding over new branches and speaking at public functions. Some priests — including Father O'Meehan — had been active supporters of Sinn Féin and the Volunteers even before to the rising. After 1916 'Sinn Féin priests' became objects of suspicion and, occasionally, targets of foul play. Second, throughout the county Sinn Féin leaders encouraged agrarian agitation, including cattle-driving and the levelling of stone fences on the property of large graziers. Thus the kinds of direct action against economic and social grievances which had been associated with the United Irish League now benefited Sinn Féin.[16]

Clerical approval, agrarian issues and 'mild coercion' created a heady leaven. Between October 1917 and July 1918 the membership of Sinn Féin branches in the West Riding alone grew from less than 700 to nearly 4,600. By contrast, the Irish Parliamentary Party all but collapsed in the county. In September 1919 the police reported that seven of the UIL's twelve branches had folded, 'the members having either gone over to Sinn Féin, or ceased to profess politics'. This last observation points to the vagaries of Sinn Féin's appeal as late as 1919: not all who joined its ranks were committed republican separatists. Some clearly were, and, like Ó Fathaigh, they were the organising corps of the party. Others were interested in very specific, longstanding economic and social aims, while still others sought a more moderate constitutional change and turned to Sinn Féin almost by default. Whatever the electors' reasons for backing the party, nationally Sinn Féin proved its mettle in December 1918, winning seventy-three seats in the United Kingdom general election. Those men and women who were not in prison in January 1919 constituted themselves as the first Dáil Éireann.[17]

Meanwhile the campaign against the police and other Crown authorities had shifted from isolation and non-recognition to direct confrontation. In August 1918 the Inspector-General of the RIC reported that 'in some lawless localities members of the Force were wantonly attacked and compelled to use their arms for self-defence'. Two months later 500 Sinn Féin supporters in Galway city broke up a meeting in support of the British military and threw rocks at the police in the street. Constables and their families received threatening letters, and young women who dated police became subject to nocturnal terror campaigns designed to discourage their associating with the RIC. Then, in January 1919, a company of Volunteers at Soloheadbeg, County Tipperary, attacked a police convoy and stole a shipment of explosives. This move touched off attacks in the south and west of Ireland in which Volunteer units — increasingly termed the Irish Republican Army — ambushed RIC men or raided barracks looking for arms. Five months later the County Inspector of Galway's East Riding recorded ominously that 'There is little open condemnation of the recent shootings of members of the Force, and any such is always accompanied by the remark that the Force is to blame.' Conditions grew so tenuous for the police that the RIC abandoned its smaller barracks in the disturbed areas early in 1920 and concentrated forces in larger district facilities. In turn, the IRA razed the empty outposts and had a freer hand in the countryside. According to a statement released by Dublin Castle in December 1920, more than 220 police and military had been killed and some 531 barracks had been destroyed since January.[18]

The conflict which developed was marked by persistent low-grade tension that erupted sporadically in intense, highly personalised violence. Non-combatants uneasily continued their daily activities amidst the actions and reactions of Crown and IRA forces. During 1919 and 1920 the composition of the opposing sides changed significantly. Generally Volunteer companies consisted of young single men who continued to work in shops or on farms by day and to march intermittently for the Republic by night. Their officers were also relatively young (with a median age of only twenty-five), though they tended to possess some social distinction in their localities: more than half of the IRA's officers were the eldest sons in their families. (Ó Fathaigh was thus somewhat exceptional, in that he was the third son in his family and considerably older than most of his fellow officers.) By the middle of 1920 he and others who were particularly well known to police left their homes and lived on the run in order to avoid capture. Congregating out of a desire for protection and companionship, they formed the nuclei of the IRA's 'flying columns' and engaged in most of the actual fighting in 1920 and 1921.

On the other hand, the British administration vacillated between conciliation, negotiation and repression. Government innovations brought police and military forces into increasingly close co-operation, to such an extent that — in David Fitzpatrick's memorable phrase — 'the hitherto distinct roles of soldier and policeman were fused, contorted, and reassorted'. Military units assisted police raiding parties, and in January 1920 the RIC and military intelligence worked up a unified list of suspects to arrest under the authority of the Defence of the Realm Act. In March recruits from Britain swelled the ranks of the RIC. Demobbed veterans of the Great War, these 'Black and Tans' were not accustomed to the regulations and traditional limits on violence implicit in a civilian police force. Then in the summer of 1920 demobilised army officers further augmented Crown forces in mobile Auxiliary units with still more firepower.

Both camps gathered information on their adversaries, but intelligence was often patchy or inaccurate, as combatants avoided falling into discernible patterns of activity. Armed confrontations were, therefore, somewhat unpredictable and consequently more memorable. From the summer of 1920, whenever IRA units did successfully attack Crown forces, their friends and families at home fell prey to brutal reprisals. Such reactions eroded enthusiasm for government policy among the British electorate, particularly when the administration tried to deny that reprisals had occurred or to portray them as attempts to control disorder. Ultimately, as the IRA remained in the field, declining support pushed the cabinet and Dublin Castle towards the truce signed in July 1921.[19]

II

Incarceration became a favoured government weapon against IRA and Sinn Féin 'suspects' in the Anglo-Irish conflict, and one of the great strengths of this memoir is Ó Fathaigh's personal account of prison life. His first experience behind bars came in 1916 when the court martial in Dublin sentenced him to penal servitude for life, later commuted to ten years. On three subsequent occasions between 1918 and 1920 he also found himself under arrest, and one can follow the development of the independence struggle by relating these events to his political and military activities.

After Ó Fathaigh's capture in 1916 the police had taken him to Limerick prison. There he found other 'Sinn Féin' prisoners already in custody. One of them may well have been the young Michael Brennan of Meelick, County Clare, who was also held in Limerick after the rising. The authorities transferred a large number of prisoners, including Brennan, from Limerick to Dublin on 9 May.[20] If they moved Ó Fathaigh at the same time, this would place him in Dublin just three days before the deaths of Séan Mac Diarmada and James Connolly signalled the end of the executions.

Several points strike the reader about Ó Fathaigh's three weeks in Dublin. First, one learns of the harsh treatment meted out to the rebels by the police and military. Forced initially to eat dog biscuits, Ó Fathaigh spent most of his time in Richmond Barracks and Kilmainham Jail. Because prisoners received only one blanket to warm themselves within Kilmainham's dank stone walls, they were probably cold as well as hungry. Moreover, one can imagine that Pádraig felt a very different kind of chill as he walked in the exercise yard, awaiting court martial, watching as soldiers washed away the blood from the executions. One also senses his apparent shock at the manner in which he and others learned of their punishment: officers stood behind them and paused for effect between announcing their full sentences and their commuted terms. One week later, on 30 May, Ó Fathaigh and a group of nine others went to Dartmoor prison to serve their sentences.[21]

During the next thirteen months he came to know many of the men who shaped the nascent Irish state, including Eamon de Valera, William Cosgrave, Thomas Ashe, Harry Boland, Austin Stack, Diarmuid Lynch and Eoin MacNeill. With an eye for close detail, Ó Fathaigh illustrates the banalities of their prison life with its work routines and tasteless meals. He also outlines how these monotonies aided the growth of mutual dependence and discipline among the Irish prisoners, who discovered ways to pass along news and circumvent prison rules. For example, the prison barbers became critical links in the chain of communication since they had contact with nearly all of their fellows. Similarly, the work detail at Dartmoor was sewing coal sacks, and each man received his material from a single member of the crew, Robert Brennan of County Wexford. Brennan worked next to a prison warder whose son edited a newspaper, the *Prison Gazette*, so he was in a position to pick up news in casual conversation and then pass it out along with the material. Moreover, when prison authorities granted the men freedom to read and study, they focused on their outside interests. Such opportunities increased after the government concentrated all of the Irish prisoners at Lewes prison in December 1916. Once there, de Valera and others organised Irish-language classes during exercise time, which led to another minor breach of prison rules. As one of the teachers, Ó Fathaigh suggested that the classes ignore a regulation about prisoners exercising only in pairs: walking in groups of four, each instructor could meet with three students at a time. When the warders did not challenge this infraction, 'Lewes prison was transformed into a Gaelic school'. Significantly, the prisoners engaged in more serious challenges, including work stoppages and the systematic destruction of cell windows, in their efforts to receive recognition as political prisoners.[22]

Whether enduring countless breakfasts of oaten gruel or serving a period of solitary confinement for refusing to work, the inmates' belief that they were part of a common struggle grew stronger with time. Paradoxically, the prison experience also encouraged a light-hearted camaraderie which sustained these men in the hard years ahead. An illustration of this latter point came at a dinner held in Loughrea in November 1917, about four and a half months after the prisoners had returned home. The guests of honour that night were de Valera, MacNeill and Francis Fahy, with de Valera delivering a speech about the need for an independent Ireland. The programme for the evening featured both ragged patriotic verse ('For our country has awakened, we have heard the trumpet blast, / The traitor's power is shattered and the sleep of slaves is past') and a bill of fare designed especially for the former 'jailbirds': dessert options included 'Rice and Marmalade Pudding à la Frongoch', 'Tipsy Cake à la Dartmoor' and 'Tricolour Jelly and Blancmange'.[23] Gallows humour was no doubt welcome sustenance for those who experienced repeated periods of imprisonment.

When he returned to Ireland in 1917, Ó Fathaigh's work again included language instruction, as well as Volunteer and IRB activities. Within days of his return, he entered party politics, assisting with de Valera's victorious parliamentary bid in a by-election in East Clare. Contrary to Ó Fathaigh's assertion in his account that this event 'meant the beginning of the end for the Irish Parliamentary Party', it was the third such victory over Redmond's forces in 1917 and part of the larger change in public opinion that was already under way. But for Ó Fathaigh, the East Clare by-election marked the beginning of the next phase of the independence struggle.

His subsequent political and military career continually placed him in compromising situations, and police detained him on three more occasions. His second arrest — which does not appear in the memoir — occurred in February 1918 near Clarinbridge. Despite his court martial, the patrol apparently did not yet know him. When questioned about his intentions, Pádraig responded only that he was a teacher. The police searched him and found a typewritten copy of the Volunteer constitution and leaflets imploring that the 'Women of Ireland Join Sinn Féin Clubs'. With no further information, the Competent Military Authority directed that he be released after one night in jail.[24]

Police next arrested Ó Fathaigh on 23 June 1919, this time for 'refusing to give any account of himself while staying in a Hotel in Mountbellew'. By then he had assumed a number of important roles in the separatist struggle. Already the Intelligence Officer for the IRA's Gort Brigade, he had also become one of the leading organisers of Sinn Féin in County Galway, raising money for the loan campaign which funded the business of Dáil Éireann. As such, he worked indirectly in two capacities for the Republican Minister for Finance and army Director of Intelligence, Michael Collins. Hoping to meet with contacts near Athenry, Ó Fathaigh had rented a room in Mountbellew because the owner of the hotel was a supporter of the UIL named Pádraig Ó Fathaigh. Thus any inquiries as to his identity might meet with confusion. When the police burst into his room, they knew only that he had signed his name in Irish in the hotel register and that the hotel owner did not know his business. Ó Fathaigh again refused to answer questions from the police, and this time he would speak to them only in Irish. When told that his lack of co-operation meant that he would be put behind bars, he refused to recognise the RIC's jurisdiction: 'Níl ceart agat é sin a dhéunamh mar ní admhuighim an Riagaltas Sasanach agus ní labharfaidh mé leat ach Gaedhilge amháin' ['You have no right to do that because I do not acknowledge English law and I will not speak anything but Irish with you']. He spent the next five days in jail.

Coming after the campaign against the RIC had turned violent, the Mountbellew arrest led to a brief moment of celebrity for Ó Fathaigh. His detention had taken place on the same day as the murder of District Inspector Michael Hunt in Thurles, one of the more brazen early attacks on an RIC man. In the following days the press paid considerable attention to Hunt's murder and to the inconclusive investigation which followed. But Father Malachy Brennan, the chairman of Sinn Féin in East Galway, wrote to the *Irish Independent* on 25 June to complain that the press was paying a disproportionate amount of attention to the Hunt shooting on the unproved — if accurate — assumption that it had been a political crime. Meanwhile, Father Brennan asserted, nothing had appeared in print about the 'outrage on our national feelings' represented by Ó Fathaigh's arrest and detention for the crime of answering the police in Irish. Father Brennan's analogy touched off an exchange of letters between himself and a correspondent who signed himself 'Co. Sligo Catholic'. This anonymous writer disparaged any comparison between Hunt's 'foul, brutal, and cowardly murder' and 'the arrest of a local petty politician' at Mountbellew. By the time the exchange concluded with a stinging reply from Father Brennan, his initial arrow had hit its mark: on 3 July the *Irish Independent* listed Ó Fathaigh among individuals 'Not Charged, But Released' by police.[25]

Ó Fathaigh's arrest at Mountbellew also created a potentially damaging situation for the Volunteers' intelligence operation in the area because he possessed detailed information about the RIC and their supplies. When the police arrested him, they found his IRA notebook, containing much of this information. Had the constabulary's shorthand expert not misread the notes — by assuming that they were in English rather than in Gaelic — the police would have realised that Ó Fathaigh had recorded the deployment of both IRA and Crown forces throughout the region. Instead, faced with expert opinion that the notes were nonsensical, they eventually released him for lack of evidence.

Having escaped serious consequences at Mountbellew, Ó Fathaigh nonetheless had caught the attention of the police. Now officially a 'suspect', 'Patrick Fahy, organiser of Sinn Féin in South & East Galway' appears in the RIC reports 'constantly travelling through the [East] Riding on his bicycle'. Still, he apparently succeeded in keeping his connection with the Dáil Loan campaign a secret. If surreptitious, this work must also have been effective because for the remainder of 1919 the frustrated police in the East Riding continually found people distributing leaflets and painting blank walls to encourage support of the loan.[26]

In January 1920 the government expanded its use of the Defence of the Realm Regulations allowing for the internment of anyone on suspicion that they had committed or would commit a crime. It was at this time that the police and military intelligence drew up the aforementioned list of suspects to be apprehended. Ó Fathaigh was almost certainly among them. In February police arrested two of his former language pupils — Michael (Mikie) Hynes and Patrick Kilkelly, both members of the IRA at Kinvara.[27] Pádraig's own capture occurred some time after this, though one of the police told him that they had been 'watching to arrest me for three weeks'. Taken initially from Kilcolgan to Gort and then to Galway and Dublin, he eventually finished up at Wormwood Scrubs in London.

Ó Fathaigh's last arrest is perhaps his most interesting for the light that it sheds on two aspects of the conflict in early 1920 — the declining morale of the constabulary before the arrival of the Black and Tans, and the growing dissatisfaction in Britain with the means used in the campaign to suppress disorder in Ireland. While held at Kilcolgan, Ó Fathaigh witnessed the profound effect that the Volunteer terror campaign had had on police discipline. Recognising that he was far from sympathetic towards the constabulary, his brief account nonetheless presents a realistic picture of men on the edge — drinking, trading blows, ignoring orders, and showing genuine regret (rather than anger) when their prisoner refused to share food or to speak with them. Moreover, Ó Fathaigh's silent boycott of the RIC stands in stark relief against his verbal sparring — in English — with his military escorts *en route* to England and his friendly relations with the prison warders at Wormwood Scrubs, emphasising the special antipathy which Irish separatists felt for the RIC.

Throughout his final detention Ó Fathaigh utilised what had become one of the most potent protests in the arsenal of republican prisoners since 1917 — the hunger-strike. Interned prisoners frequently resorted to the hunger-strike in an attempt to secure either trials or recognition as political prisoners. Beginning on 5 April 1920 at Mountjoy Prison, for example, republican internees engaged in one of the most famous large-scale hunger-strikes of the period. Lasting ten days, the strike inspired daily demonstrations outside the prison, as well as condemnations from the Catholic hierarchy and a one-day general strike by Irish labour which was almost universal outside of Belfast. It also coincided with the appointment of a new Irish Chief Secretary, Sir Hamar Greenwood, and a new commander of British military forces in Ireland, Sir Nevil Macready. Faced with a vast public outcry, the new administration released the interned prisoners on 15 April and more clearly defined the rights which would be accorded to political prisoners in the future.[28] This rather hurried act of clemency took on a note of farce, when prison officials also released some convicted prisoners along with the internees. Just one week later the prisoners at Wormwood Scrubs began their own, less documented hunger-strike.

The strike which started on 21 April was not the first hunger protest at 'the Scrubs' that spring. In March several prisoners, including the labour leader William O'Brien, had gone on strike to object to the isolation of Joseph McGrath at Brixton prison. (The government later moved four other prisoners to Brixton to join McGrath.) Ó Fathaigh arrived shortly after this earlier incident, on 12 April, and during the period when the prisoners' committee contemplated a second strike. Committee members were divided about whether or not a strike should take place at all, possibly because their demand was new: unconditional release rather than a change in prisoner status. In his Irish-language memoir Ó Fathaigh explains that those looking to delay the strike were among his closest associates. Led by Jim Lawless, whom he had met in Dartmoor in 1916, they included Patrick Kilkelly of Kinvara and Larry Lardner of Athenry. Ó Fathaigh says that his own inclination was to participate immediately, but Kilkelly asked him to wait for a few days, at which point 'go d-téidheadh siad ar fad ar Stailc' ['they all would go on strike']. When the first prisoners refused their food, Ó Fathaigh remained with Lawless's group, though they joined the protest a few days later. By 26 April all 174 Irish prisoners at Wormwood Scrubs and the five housed at Brixton were on hunger-strike.[29]

The prisoners' action touched off republican-inspired demonstrations throughout Britain which were similar to those sparked by the Mountjoy protest earlier in the month. This time, however, they led to violent clashes with unsympathetic Britons and the police. Members of the Irish Self-Determination League and several thousand demonstrators surrounded the prison each evening, saying the rosary in Irish, singing patriotic songs, and denouncing the government's Irish policies. On at least two occasions, on 27 and 29 April, Londoners attacked the crowd and injured at least seventy people. *The Times* reported that mounted police had had to break up the latter fracas. Another account of this same clash in the *Sunday Independent* claimed that some of the police had aided the attack, boasting that 'we gave them hell; we knocked dozens of them out'. Meanwhile, on 27 April in Glasgow, police had prohibited a protest meeting in George Square organised by that city's branch of the Irish Self-Determination League. When the League defied the order, police charged the crowd with drawn batons and arrested one of the speakers. On that same day a deputation led by the local president of the League in Liverpool informed the Lord Mayor that up to 200,000 Irish workers in the city would go on strike unless the internees were released within two days. Their threat raised concern in the House of Commons and led to an extended discussion on 28 April. In the event, only 2,000 men actually stopped work, but their small numbers were offset by the impact the strike made on shipping. Among the strikers were some 200 to 300 coalheavers who refused to fuel vessels bound for Ireland, and their participation resulted in the suspension of 'practically all shipping between Ireland and Liverpool' until 4 May.[30]

Throughout the last week of April and the first part of May, amid staged demonstrations, the government faced serious questions in parliament about its use of internment. The Keeper of the Privy Seal, Andrew Bonar Law, and the Home Secretary, Edward Shortt, were adamant that the police and military in Ireland had acted lawfully to restore order and that the prisoners would remain as comfortable as possible and would not perish through lack of food. But internment was authorised through unexpired wartime legislation applicable throughout the United Kingdom, and Labour MP James Sexton voiced concern about its use *within* Britain. During the debate on 28 April he cited the case of two dock workers in Liverpool who had been seized two weeks earlier and 'taken to the military barracks at Seaforth, and from there spirited away, no one knows where, neither relatives nor mates'.[31]

Opposition MPs also raised questions about the conditions inside Wormwood Scrubs, but government spokesmen retorted that the prisoners idled their time away playing billiards. Certainly Ó Fathaigh's account supports the contention that conditions within Wormwood Scrubs were generally comfortable when he arrived. 'It was', he writes, 'as if the Government meant to kill Sinn Féin with kindness.' But according to prisoners' statements after the strike, the situation changed when a new governor arrived at the prison in early April. Outside observers also had a vague sense that conditions had changed when, in mid-April, prison officials began to turn away relatives seeking to visit internees — a violation of the conditions affirmed for political prisoners after the Mountjoy strike. As the strike dragged on, stories filtered out that prison officials had abused their charges.

It appears beyond question that some abuse did occur, but the prisoners' actions were also clearly provocative. The key nights in question were 26 and 27 April, when some prisoners smashed windows to communicate with the crowd outside; meanwhile others knocked cell doors off their hinges — ostensibly to ventilate the rooms for their weakening comrades. Ó Fathaigh accomplished this latter feat by wedging a copy of the New Testament between the frame and hinges and then throwing himself repeatedly against the door. Military guards ushered men back to their cells at the point of fixed bayonets, after which the governor ordered their removal to a basement wing of the prison to prevent further contact with their supporters outside the walls. Other alleged incidents ranged in severity from the looting of prisoners' cells to outright beatings. In one particularly dramatic claim, a warder reportedly sat on a prisoner named Crawley, breaking his denture and forcing a portion of it down his throat.[32]

Acknowledging that the Mountjoy internees had been released and that the 1916 internees had had their cases reviewed by judicial advisory committees, Home Secretary Shortt appeared receptive to the suggestion that a special review body should be established. He also noted that the internees already possessed the right to appeal for judicial reviews. What Shortt did not say was that advisory committees only made recommendations to the Home Office about whether or not to release prisoners; thus the decision ultimately rested with him. And his opinion about releasing the internees was unequivocal — 'The one object that we have is to prevent them from returning to Ireland.'[33]

By the middle of May, when calls for a review body disappeared from the House of Commons, events had taken a dramatic turn. Since late April prison officials transferred weakening hunger-strikers to hospitals around London. Their status while in hospital, however, remains unclear. Earlier published accounts have suggested that the government simply let prisoners go after they had returned to health, since most of them returned to Ireland over the next five weeks. Ó Fathaigh maintains that their situation was less certain than that. When the government removed him to St Marylebone infirmary on 8 May, he learned that the Irish would go back to prison after they had sufficiently recovered. Throughout May, when other hospitalised internees applied for their personal effects intending to leave for Ireland, the Home Office directed them back to the prison, where they were told 'that if they would give a guarantee to take food they would be admitted and kept there until such time as the authorities saw fit to send them home'.

Ultimately several former internees turned to the Irish Self-Determination League for the resources to go home.[34]

Still others, including Ó Fathaigh, adopted a more direct approach: on Sunday 16 May they simply walked out of the hospital with the aid of London sympathisers. Contrary to Ó Fathaigh's belief that only the Marylebone detainees escaped, some forty others also left the Metropolitan Hospital and the St James Infirmary, Wandsworth. Described as the 'Hunger Strikers' Coup' by the *Irish Independent*, this action created 'consternation' in the Home Office and the Irish Office. The manner in which Ó Fathaigh and the other former prisoners were 'advised to leave for Ireland immediately' suggests that they believed their situation remained precarious in London. In the event, those who left hospital like Ó Fathaigh disappeared through the London Irish and back to Ireland. By the middle of June the government acknowledged simply that most of the Wormwood Scrubs prisoners had 'secured their liberty'.[35]

The ultimate ramifications of the Wormwood Scrubs hunger-strike and escape would not be fully apparent for several months. Since 1916 hunger-strikes had forced the government to adopt any number of strategies — from application of the 'Cat and Mouse Act' to forcible feeding and to temporary grants of political prisoner status. Now, after the government had responded to public outcry by freeing the Mountjoy prisoners, the Wormwood Scrubs prisoners had ratcheted up the usual Irish demand from political prisoner status to unconditional release. When this was denied them, they had taken matters into their own hands, freeing themselves from their hospital beds. In turn, the Government announced a dramatically more austere attitude towards hunger-striking on 23 June. Henceforth, anyone who went on hunger-strike would have to face the full consequences of their action. As the world witnessed in September and October 1920, in the cases of Terence McSwiney, Michael Fitzgerald and Joseph Murphy, the government was indeed prepared to let them perish.[36]

Taken together, then, Ó Fathaigh's four arrests shed some useful light on the hidden battlefields of the Irish War of Independence — internment camps and prisons. Whether arrested for carrying suspicious papers, wearing the Volunteer uniform, expressing views sympathetic to independence, or engaging in actual combat, thousands of men and women became subject to conviction or internment between 1916 and 1921. In response, many Irish prisoners used whatever means were at their disposal to deny the right of their captors to hold them — from work stoppages to destruction of prison property and to hunger-strikes. Their more sensational tactics may have raised questions about the justification for arrests and internments, but they did not end the use of detention as a weapon in the Anglo-Irish War. Until December 1921 as many as 7,000 Irish men and women remained in prisons or internment camps. Although removed from the actual fighting, Irish prisoners nonetheless continued to play an important role in creating the stalemate of July 1921: in addition to occupying the equivalent of eight battalions of men as guards, their very presence nagged at the public conscience in Britain, eroding support for a major component of the government's Irish strategy.[37]

III

In June 1920 Ó Fathaigh rejoined the fight against the reinforced RIC in Counties Galway and Clare. His insights into the conduct of the Anglo-Irish War are considerable. While the underground Dáil sought to establish its own legitimacy in Dublin, provincial IRA units faced the elemental task of survival. The longer that they could remain in the field, the greater the chance that their undefined Republic would become a reality. Possessing only minimal resources — the IRA's lack of guns and ammunition was a persistent problem — companies depended on stealth to avoid capture and to attack Crown forces. Thus information became an invaluable weapon in their limited arsenal.

Ó Fathaigh's duties as Intelligence Officer for the Gort Brigade, therefore, carried enormous responsibility and placed him in a position to record the actions of both sides in the conflict. His contacts included men and women who socialised with politically active Unionists, as well as people who worked in post offices and railway stations from Galway city to Limerick. In developing his network, he benefited from his years of travel throughout the region because political friends and former students put him in touch with well-placed informants. One example is the so-called 'Manageress of [the] K hotel' in Galway city. The cousin of an acquaintance from County Mayo, this Miss Walshe provided Ó Fathaigh with photographs and stories about the Auxiliaries based at Lenaboy Barracks. Another critical informant was Constable Patrick Durkan of Kilcolgan, who met Ó Fathaigh in 1918 after a former student approached him with a 'poem in her praise' which Durkan had written. Over time Durkan supplied Ó Fathaigh with data about individual RIC men as well as deciphered codes and secret service reports. On one notable occasion late in 1920 he risked his own life to warn Ó Fathaigh and four others away from a potential trap.

Durkan's action underlines the dangerous game played by messengers and informants. Since one camp's sources were the other camp's spies, those who were found out usually forfeited their lives. For example, Patrick Joyce, a National Teacher from Barna, County Galway, 'disappeared' on 15 October 1920 after the IRA discovered that he was sending a list of Sinn Féiners' names and addresses to police and Dublin Castle authorities. Another case involved one of Ó Fathaigh's longtime comrades from the Volunteers, Joe Howley of Oranmore. Howley acted as a courier from the South Galway IRA to headquarters in Dublin. On 4 December 1920 a special unit of the RIC known as the 'Igoe gang' killed him shortly after he arrived at Broadstone Station in Dublin. A final potential case mentioned in the memoir was the death of Constable Kearney after the Ballyturin ambush in May 1921. Sent there to help police investigate, Kearney was shot, Ó Fathaigh suggests, by a Black and Tan. Since Kearney was one of Ó Fathaigh's sources of information about the Auxiliaries, this explanation sounds plausible, though it should be noted that the RIC believed that the IRA was responsible.[38]

Such events were, however, more the exception than the rule, as both sides developed strategies designed to frustrate their adversaries. Ambushes in Galway and Clare repeatedly failed because police or military patrols did not appear when they were expected. Between

November 1920 and June 1921 in Mid-Clare alone, one author has noted that 'Volunteers set 144 traps for the enemy, but on 130 occasions they failed to get so much as a clear sight of their quarry'.[39] At the same time, Ó Fathaigh's active service unit instructed local IRA companies about road-cutting and other techniques which disrupted Crown communications and allowed the IRA to remain viable.

Crown and IRA violence did, however, escalate after the Auxiliaries arrived in the summer of 1920. Increasingly the press reported Irish 'outrages' — such as the ambushing of police patrols — being met with Crown 'reprisals'. In December 1920 a commission established by the British Labour Party to investigate Irish conditions observed that police and military patrols rode through towns in open lorries with their rifles 'at the ready', accentuating uncertainty for non-combatants. 'The sight of "tin hats", drawn bayonets, and revolvers, and here and there of sandbags, or machine guns, or powerful searchlights, is calculated', they concluded, 'to terrorise the civilian population.'[40]

One could cite numerous incidents calculated to frighten civilians in County Galway. On 24 September, for example, police set fire to several buildings in Ardrahan, including the parish hall which Edward Martyn had built for Gaelic League functions. Throughout the autumn the playwright and folklorist Lady Gregory heard stories emanating from Peterswell to Kinvara about police patrols taking young men and boys from their homes at night and flogging them, and newspapers reported that the Black and Tans forced young men and women to run through the streets of their villages under volleys of rifle fire.[41]

Two of the more notorious incidents occurred in November 1920. On the first of the month police driving near Gort killed Mrs Eileen Quinn while she sat on the fence in front of her house. Not active politically, Mrs Quinn was both pregnant and holding an infant son when she was shot. Sir Hamar Greenwood told the House of Commons that the police 'had every right to anticipate ambushes and to prevent surprises' in Ireland 'and especially in Galway'. However, at the ensuing military court of inquiry — which refused to take statements from the parish priest or the local doctor who had heard the dying woman identify the police as her assailants — constables acknowledged that they *routinely* shot into the air while on patrol. Officially the inquiry determined that the police had fired their weapons as a precautionary measure and that Mrs Quinn's fate resulted from 'death by misadventure'.[42]

Two weeks later, on the night of 14 November, Father Michael Griffin of Rahoon parish disappeared while answering a sick call. Searchers found his body six days later in a bog with a bullet wound through his right temple. District Inspector Cruise of the RIC maintained that his men — most of whom were Catholics — would never harm a priest, and again, in the House of Commons, Greenwood deflected suspicion from any British forces. Subsequent investigation showed that Father Griffin had been taken to the military headquarters at Taylor's Hill. An inquiry into his death determined officially that the gunshot had been fired 'feloniously, wilfully and with malice', but no one identified the assailant. According to an account published later by the commander of the Auxiliary forces, the shooter was a member of the Auxiliaries, but a representative from Dublin Castle had ordered that the inquiry remain inconclusive.[43]

The Griffin case was a *cause célèbre*, but it was only the most blatant example of aggression against clergy in the diocese. Local residents recalled that Father Griffin had lived with the activist Sinn Féin priest, Father J. W. O'Meehan, and that Crown forces had raided their home five times in the months before Griffin's disappearance. In September, when the government established a curfew in the county, copies of the curfew notice had appeared on the door of their residence in the shape of a cross, underneath which someone had inscribed the words 'Doomed. RIP. Amen.' Then, on 25 November, Bishop Thomas O'Dea of Galway wrote an open letter to the Chief Secretary protesting that he and several of his priests had received letters threatening them with 'Father Griffin's fate'. Among the cases highlighted by the bishop was that of the parish priest of Gort, Father Considine, who had received a letter asserting that 'Your efforts to stir up the blood-lust against the Crown forces are duly noted. You will be duly compensated, as will all the friends of the hero, Michael Collins.' Father Considine's only offence, according to the bishop, had been publishing his opinion about Mrs Quinn's death earlier in the month. Father Considine took the threat seriously and asked his parishioners not to bring sick calls to him after dark. Lest one assume that the public viewed all Crown forces as acting maliciously towards him, however, it should be noted that eight veteran constables responded to the priest's fears by protecting his home whenever Black and Tans drove through Gort.[44]

Indeed, while Ó Fathaigh states that some members of the 'old' RIC engaged in terror tactics alongside the Black and Tans, he also records that others were 'inoffensive' during the conflict. One of his informants, Constable McDermott, prevented the Black and Tans from burning the home of the woman who acted as his contact with Ó Fathaigh. Another constable intervened when Ó Fathaigh's brother Mícheál was about to be arrested by the Auxiliaries. Given the generally embittered relations between the constabulary and Sinn Féin activists, however, the most exceptional case Ó Fathaigh cites was that of his host family at Carran, County Clare — the Difflys. Mrs Diffly was a Gaelic enthusiast with two sons, a sister and other near relations who were 'ardent' Sinn Féiners and IRA officers; meanwhile her husband was a sergeant serving in the RIC in County Galway.

A final aspect of the independence struggle which Ó Fathaigh highlights is the tit-for-tat nature of its violence. He provides, for example, some important background material concerning the gruesome murders of Patrick and Harry Loughnane of Shanaglish in December 1920. Pat Loughnane, an IRA captain and the president of the local Sinn Féin branch, had been involved in an ambush of police at Castledaly in October, which alone might have marked him as a target. He later killed a retired police sergeant in a hand-to-hand fight and subsequently embarrassed the dead man's son who had come looking for revenge. According to Ó Fathaigh, the son was also an officer in the Auxiliaries, and it was these events which led to the Loughnanes' arrest.

The clearest example of reprisal targeting in the memoir is the one which affected Ó Fathaigh most directly — even though he only learned of it after the fact. This was the burning of his family home by Crown forces on 15 May 1921 in response to the IRA's successful ambush of a tennis party at Ballyturin. The main target at Ballyturin was the English-born Captain C. E. N. Blake, who took over as the RIC's District Inspector in Gort about the time that Pádraig left to join the Mid-Clare Brigade. Blake cultivated a reputation as 'a terror', boasting to acquaintances in England that he would go to Ireland 'to make it hot'. Within weeks of his arrival, Lady Gregory's daughter-in-law Margaret remonstrated with him, objecting to what she considered state-sponsored mayhem. This same Margaret Gregory was the sole survivor of the Ballyturin ambush, the IRA having spared her apparently because of her family affiliation. The rest of the party, including Blake, his wife and two military officers, each received at least four bullet wounds in the meticulously planned and executed operation.[45]

As prominent local republicans, the Ó Fathaigh family had already endured the attention of Crown authorities before the Ballyturin incident. Blake and his men had searched the family home repeatedly looking for Pádraig. On one such occasion they arrested Mícheál Ó Fathaigh and took him to Galway jail, where he remained for a short time. Moreover, on the morning of 15 May, before the tennis party went to Ballyturin, police and military forces had baton-charged and scattered the nearly 700 mourners marching to the funeral of Pádraig's sister Mary, who had died on the preceding day.

In the wake of the ambush, though, police attention literally flared up at Lurgan. As Ó Fathaigh's other siblings gathered after Mary's funeral, word came from a neighbour that they should vacate the premises. Shortly afterwards Crown forces descended, setting fire to the house and outbuildings and to the homes of two neighbours. They then proceeded into Gort, where they raided six houses, burnt another, and set fire to a granary. One witness told the *Irish Independent* that 'before dawn the scene in the neighbourhood was like a sunset glow, the horizon being fringed with the flames from the burning houses'.[46]

The persistence of such actions by both camps into the early summer of 1921 furthered the disillusionment of the British public already noted in relation to incarceration. Critically, the efforts by Crown forces to stamp out Sinn Féin and the IRA did nothing to endear the government to the vast majority of Irish people. Indeed, outside of the six counties in Ulster which received their own devolved parliament through the Government of Ireland Act of 1920, most Irish non-combatants either tacitly supported the push for independence or hoped for a peaceful end to the conflict. Ultimately the Dáil and the British cabinets agreed to a truce which took effect on 11 July, and their representatives then negotiated the Articles of Agreement, which were signed on 6 December 1921.

IV

In the last section of the memoir we see Ó Fathaigh continuing to work for his notion of the Republic during the latter part of 1921 and the uncertain early months of 1922. After the truce he returned to County Galway and to his work as an Intelligence Officer, earning congratulations for his efforts from Michael Collins himself. When the Articles of Agreement failed, in Pádraig's eyes, to recognise the Republic for which he had fought, he spoke out against adoption of 'the Treaty'. Despite his efforts, opinions on the Treaty seemed almost evenly divided in south Galway. It is a pity that Ó Fathaigh does not include more information about this period, because what he does report hints at the emergence of the same kinds of divisions between allies that marked the more famous disputes in Dublin. Some of his longtime Volunteer and Sinn Féin comrades — like George Nicholls — were pro-Treaty, suggesting that greater detail might have clarified the development of post-Civil War parties in the county.

Ó Fathaigh's public life after the Civil War continued to revolve around his commitment to traditional Irish culture and his understanding of republican ideals. He married a schoolteacher, Maighréad Ní Chonaing, in September 1922, and they settled at Tullira, Ardrahan, where they raised five children. Pádraig earned a degree in Celtic Studies from University College, Galway, and taught Irish in summer colleges and at Gaelic League branches in Peterswell, Ardrahan and

Ballyturin. When these classes fell under the direction of the Technical Committee of the County Council in the 1920s, he taught without pay rather than take the oath of allegiance required under the Anglo-Irish Treaty. In 1936, when Gort hosted the regional Feis Connacht, he served as secretary of the planning committee and secured a visit from de Valera to the festivities. For a time he worked as a clerk in the Health Board Section of the Galway County Council, and during years of petrol shortage he made the daily forty-mile trip to work on his trusted bicycle. Ever the organiser, he served as National Secretary to the 'Old Comrades IRA', and in the early 1950s he was secretary of the committee which arranged for a monument to Liam Mellows in Eyre Square in Galway city.[47]

D'éag Pádraig Ó Fathaigh 19 Feabhra 1976.

Editorial Note

Ó Fathaigh's writing is generally coherent and clear, though his text contains a number of misspellings (most notably of the names of persons and places) and his use of punctuation and capitalisation was not consistent. While I have generally retained these errors and inconsistencies, I have occasionally supplied additional punctuation in order to avoid obscurity. For the same reason, I have added some obviously missing letters to words within square brackets; inverted commas have been supplied in all instances of direct speech; and the titles of books and newspapers have been given in italic type. Occasional brief explanations and clarifications of obscuritites have been given within square brackets.

Readers will note that certain oddities in Ó Fathaigh's spelling and use of abbreviation remain. For example, he occasionally wrote the names of friends in their Irish form in one place and in English elsewhere, so that one will find both Colm *Ó Gaora* and *O'Geary*. He also utilised the time-honoured technique of concealing the identity of individuals by spelling out only their initials or a portion of their names, especially when writing about his informants or his political opponents. Wherever possible, I have identified such people in footnotes at the relevant points in the text. Lastly, military abbreviations are also common, such as 'coy' for company or 'adjt' for adjutant. To avoid cluttering the text unduly, I have expanded these designations on their first appearance in the text and have generally left them as abbreviations thereafter.

Pádraig Ó Fathaigh

Memoir
1968

After advent of Irish Volunteers, drill was taught by me at Ballyglass, Castledaly, Ardrahan & Skehanagh (Peterswell) in addition to Gaelic & Irish dancing. When Liam Mellows[1] came as Volunteer Organizer, he visited these Irish classes. His headquarters was at Athenry, but he also had his tent in Ballycahalan from which he organized and trained the companies in the Gort Battallion area.

The Volunteer activities in county were directed by the Galway County Board Irish Volunteers. With Captain Mellows as organizer, George Nichols, chairman, Joe Howley treasurer, Pádraig Ó Fathaigh Secretary & Larry Lardner, Brigade Commandant.[2] The Irish classes gave a great philip [*fillip*] to the Volunteer movement, through the national spirit it awakened in the people, and Captain Mellow[s]'s success left the RIC amazed and bewildered.

I was one of the delegates at the Limerick Convention when arrangements were made for the Rising on Easter Sunday.[3] The arms (expected) were to be sorted at Abbeyfeale, a portion kept and a quantity sent by train to Gort for the arming of the Galway Volunteers.

The Ballycahalan Coy [Company] and others mobilized armed at Ballylee, when a dispatch arrived stating that the Easter Sunday manoeuvres were countermanded by Owen McNeill.[4] Comdt [Commandant] Mellows escaped from Reading Detention area & came in disguise to Killeeneen. The Gort meeting for Easter Monday had been cancelled unknown to Capt Mellows (now promoted to Comdt) and the huge concourse who came to Gort were bewildered & disappointed and soaked in Rain.

Near Killeeneen I met Fr Feeney[5] who informed me that Dublin was out and that Galway was going out on Tuesday morning The night was spent preparing; making bombs etc and before day Comdt Mellows asked me to go to Gort district, & get Ballycahalan and other companies to mobilize and remain in Gort area. I asked him then if I would go by Kinvara and bring Fr O'Meehan[6] to organize the food supplies. After a long pause he said, 'Go to Kinvara & bring Fr O'Meehan back to Killeeneen' (he himself wanted him as qr master).

He sent Tom O'Dea with me, & an Athenry man was with the driver. It happened that a rumour went round that arms were being landed at Kinvara, and Fr O'Meehan was warned to keep away as the RIC were alerted.

Tom O'Dea wanted to fire at Kilcolgan Barracks, but on reaching Kinvara he noticed the RIC car. And on reaching Kinvara Lodge, where Fr O'Meehan resided, Tom O'Dea & myself were confronted by 2 armed RIC men in the darkness. O'Dea explained that we were on a sick call, that he was Donoghue from Dooras and I also gave a fictitious name. By this time the RIC man separated from the sergeant and had his rifle ready, and as we were about to enter the car, O'Dea was arrested & the RIC man shouted 'whoever stirs a foot I'll shoot him dead'. I went to O'Dea's aid and tried to take the rifle from the sergeant. The latter shouted to the constable to come to his assistance. The RIC man let go O'Dea and I managed to struggle with both & I shouted to O'Dea for help. O'Dea who had gained the car was rushing back when the RIC man who managed to break loose from me pointed the rifle at O'Dea, the latter got into the car and I thought I saw him open door & fire back. The RIC man fired on the moving car and then called on me to let go the sergeant who by this time was completely exhausted. Putting the rifle to my back he gave me ten seconds to put up my hands which I did at the count of nine. It was some time before the sergeant could proceed — from exhaustion

In the black hole, when sergeant appeared with my coat he began to question me, and when I answered him in Irish he got very angry and took away my coat again.

Suddenly a constable rushed in to the Barracks saying the rebels had a machine gun outside every barrack in county, that the smaller barracks were being evacuated, that Ardrahan were preparing to evacuate and when they reached Kinvara, Kinvara was to evacuate and all were to hasten to Gort.

Ardrahan peelers soon arrived and the panic spread: Constable McBirney, who was about to bring me tea, flung his rifle against the ground saying he was finished with the RIC.

The RIC fled helter skelter to Gort, expecting to be attacked on the way. I was on a sidecar handcuffed.

After a long consultation at Gort Barracks I was placed in a motor-car & driven to Limerick RIC Barracks, under a strong RIC Guard, so many that the tyres burst near Ennis. Some RIC men were brought in to the large lock-up in Limerick where I was lodged & made swear on their knees that they would carry out their orders, & a police officer went down on his knees cursing me.

There were some Sinn Féin Prisoners in Limerick Jail when I arrived there, but after a day I was isolated from the other prisoners, until after the surrender when we were marched to the Railway Station and taken to Richmond Barracks. We got one rug for blanket and slept on the bare floor and for food dog biscuits until the arrival of Asquith[7] when good food was supplied

Court Martial

On a Saturday, I with John Coen[8] was brought out for courtmartial. Mr Coen was sent back and I was tried. The DI and the Sergeant & Constable who arrested me gave evidence, the latter stating that he knew me to be a Sinn Féin organizer & saw me with Capt Mellows. A man from the locality also testified that I swore him in to be true to his country, but did not know if it was the IRB oath.

The DI pressed the General to finish the case on Saturday, but the General pointed out that the case would take a full day. Then the DI said he would be satisfied with a summary of the charges, but the General said that he could not deal with even a summary as there were so many charges. Then he appealed to the Court Martial to take the case the 1st on Monday morning. The DI wanted to rush the trial as he feared Asquith's visit would halt the executions and long-term sentences

On Monday I was ordered out with John Curran & outside was Colm O'Geary[9] and the informer. Because of the inability of the Englishman to pronounce *r* there was a blunder. Curran was pronounced Coen. Curran was taken back to Richmond, but in the meantime John Coen was deported to England. The DI, Sergeant Reilly, Const[able] McCarthy, Constable McKeown and the informer gave evidence.

Mr O'Brien-Moran my solicitor was not allowed to defend me. He made me tare [*tear*] up the statement admitting I was in the Sinn Féin Volunteers, said that my case was very serious & not to admit anything but let them prove it. Then a military officer stepped forward & volunteered to defend me. I declined. The DI Serg[ean]t Reilly, McCarthy & the informer repeated their evidence of Saturday. Constable McKeown swore that I was a Sinn Féin organizer, that Captain Mellows stayed at my house for weeks at a time as also Captain Frank Fahy[10] who had been recently sentenced. The General asked was Captain Mellows a military officer or a rebel captain: the DI answered 'a rebel captain and a fugitive from Justice'.

'Then why have you not him here?' was the stinging retort.

'Unfortunately he eluded us' was the muttered answer.

I got a surprize when the DI was asked for my character outside of politics. He said 'I have to admit that I could not find the least thing against his character. I inquired from every place he frequented and all were unanimous that his character was exemplary.'

The RIC were most bitter and vindictive, on the other hand the military, both Irish & English & Scotch were friendly and sympathetic. On being taken to Kilmainham I waved to pals Vol[unteer]s who were at a window in Richmond Barracks. The officer shouted 'Hit him on the head with the rifle.' But the soldiers did not obey the command.

A similar incident occured in 1920, as I was being taken through Dublin. A woman said 'Go mbeannuidhe Dia dhuit.' I answered 'Dia is Muire Dhuit.'[11] 'Hit him in the head with the rifle' roared Lt Wedgewood. The Cameron Highlander whispered to me to say nothing.

The disused Kilmainham Prison was full of dust and a number were put together in each cell. We were given porridge for supper, but there could be as much salt as porridge and soon everybody was shouting for water. This could have been a trick of Corporal Mons an English soldier who said to a Volunteer (myself) 'It would be a waste of water to give you a drink, as you will be shot in the morning.' He went round to the prisoners soliciting tips. Michael Fleming[12] gave him a 10/– note to bring him food, but the corporal brought back neither food nor money. We slept on the bare prison floor that night. Next morning we were given blankets to bring out and shake in prison yard. We were shown where the executions took place. Some soldiers with brushes were sweeping away the blood stains and applying Jey[es]'s fluid to the ground. We were shown the chair where Connolly[13] sat when he wrenched off the back rail. The wall beside which the executed Volunteers stood was riddled with bullet marks. The sergeant, of Irish Rifles I think, also showed us where the Invincibles were buried,[14] but their numbers had been recently removed & their graves were merely indicated by fresh mortar marks in the wall. The sergeant was very loquacious and friendly with McNeill, whilst Peter Slattery's charming manner seemed to captivate him. He asserted that Séan Heuston[15] was as brave a man as ever walked. The lads of the firing squad seemed to admire and fear him, and the rifles actually fell on the ground. The sergeant himself was not sympathetic; he condemned the Rising and averred that if he were in authority, he too would have Heuston executed, because in 25 years' time, Heuston if alive would be there to let loose another rebellion.

The Sentences

We were marched out to the prison yard to hear our sentences. Some officers approached me and read to me my sentence. It was penal servitude for life. After a long pause the officer said this had been confirmed, by the CO [Commanding Officer] and then after a very long pause, He said, 'This has been commuted to Ten years PS [penal servitude].' Colm O'Geary was nearby. I whispered to him asking what was his sentence. He said 15 years. I said 'I do not believe it.' 'I hardly believed my ears myself. Perhaps it was 15 months, but they couldn't reduce 15 months to 10 years,' Colm said.

Connolly & McDermott[16] proved to be the last executed in Kilmainham. We were marched back to Mountjoy Jail. Mountjoy was similar to Limerick, cells 8' × 4', floors & walls clean, food poor in quality and quantity. We were employed sewing bags which was light easy work.

One day a soldier whispered to me, 'Ye are being sent to Dartmoor. There is where the other prisoners were sent.' I told Mr Fleming, but he would not believe it.

Next day we were hand cuffed and marched through Dublin Numbers of children cheered wildly until we were put in the Black Maria, a long narrow vehicle in which it was difficult to turn around. Put on board a vessel we danced and sang and made merry. I think it was 8 prisoners that was in this batch including McNeill, Slattery, M. Fleming, J. Corcoran and some Oranmore men. We were in [the] charge of a Coy of Dublin Fusiliers under Capt. Macnamara of Tulla, Co. Clare. At Hol[l]yhead a soldier asked permission to see me. He was a Connacht Ranger name[d] Fallon from Ballinasloe. He was sympathetic, but a girl who was with him said, 'These from Galway should be all shot.' The Fusiliers were friendly and gave us water to drink. The Connacht Rangers were not allowed to go with prisoners They had been sent with a contingent, and came back mad drunk.

Near Dartmoor, at Princetown perhaps, a crowd consisting of warders' wives and sons and daughter[s] collected and began to scan the prisoners. Capt. Macnamara asked them to move away. 'These' he said 'are the warders' wives & children and they wish ye no good.' 'Go quick' he said 'or I'll order a bayonet charge.' They disappeared.

'Against that' he said 'it was the women of Manchester who were first to cry out against the executions. I know this as I was in Manchester at the time.'

The soldiers cheered us up, saying the Dartmoor warders were not brutal. Do not give trouble, do what you are asked, and do not attempt to talk.

Dartmoor

There is no prison the 'jail Birds' dread more than Dartmoor. Built in a wild desolate mountain moor. During 5 days out of 7 it is enveloped in a thick fog and the other two days raining (perhaps) with a stinging East wind.

In a hall the eight Prisoners were searched and checked over, warned and cautioned by officials warders etc. who seemed more stern and exacting than those in Irish prisons. Next, each prisoner was taken to a bath and subjected to the naked search, including the hair, under the tongue etc. Taken to the exercise yard next morning in our own clothes. A number of prisoners marched quickly around in files 6 paces apart. Dressed in k[h]aki with nickers & round caps. At first glance I imagined these were Turkish prisoners of war. But as we came along with McNeill in front, the tallest of the gang shouted, 'Irish Volunteers; attention; eyes right; dismiss.' The prisoners obeyed the orders of their Leader, de Valera[17] and the salute was for Eoin McNeill. It was like a bomb. For a time there was consternation among the warders. Then a prison official said, 'Take him back to his cell.' De Valera was hurried to his cell but was allowed out to exercise again next morning The Irish prisoners were housed in a wing of Dartmoor prison away from the other criminals. It was here the French Prisoners of war were kept, and they died like flies.

The walls and floors are of grey granite. The cells 8' × 4'. Portion of the door underneath consists of strong wire netting to allow air. There is a stool, and a board inserted in the angle of the wall does duty for a table. There is also gaslight whilst at the other end is a window; well barred. There is a plank for bed, with two rough linen sheets, two small blankets & a rug.

The Food

The food is very bad. During 1st month, breakfast consisted of 4 ozs brown loaf with pint of skilly, supper 4 ozs brown loaf with cocoa. In contrast to the other articles of food, this cocoa is excellent. Dinner varies, each day having its special food. Monday 4 ozs Norwegian bacon (all fat) with potatoes. Tuesday 5 ozs beef & potatoes. Wednesday pea soup. Thursday 5 ozs mutton with potatoes. Friday vegetable soup. Saturday Bread pudding. Sunday a few slices of Bully Beef. Beef and mutton are hard as leather, potatoes have patches of dry rot, sometimes substituted by the large unnutritious white turnip The water is bog water, and is undrinkable except when treated with oatmeal.

Work

For the 1st month the prisoners were confined to their cells, and the work consisted of sewing bags, which was easy. The hours were, getting up at 6 new time, fixing your bed showing your sheets to the warder etc. Then 20 minutes exercise, and search. Back then to breakfast, dinner at midday, supper after exercise & to bed at 8. After one month solitary, the prisoners were taken to a large workshop. There were 3 rows of forms, there were 4 persons in each form in centre row and 3 in each of the outer rows. Prisoners sitting 3 feet apart & silent. A warder stood in front of each row and a chief warder stood behind the 3 rows.

The work was making naval coal sacks, and the bread ration was increased to 5 oz brown loaf (or bun)

The Prisoners

There were 65 Sinn Féin Prisoners in Dartmoor including de Valera. 14 from Oranmore: Iodhan & Joe Howley, Eddie Corcoran, Mick Higgins, Jim Loughlin, Joe Burke, 3 Furies, 2 Carricks, M. Hehir M. Flanagan, P. Toole, W. Corcoran. 3 from Clarinbridge: Ml Fleming, Jonny Corcoran, W. Hussy. These with Brian Molloy, Castlegar, Colm O'Geary, Rosmuck & myself made 20 from County Galway. 7 from Wexford: Seán Etchingham, Séamus Doyle, Bob Brennan, Mick de Lacy, Seumas Wrafter, J. Donohue and John Tomkins. 4 from Kerry: Austin Stack, Desmond Fitzgerald, Fionán Lynch, Tadg Brosnan. 3 from Limerick — Con Collins, Peter Slattery, Dr Hayes. 4 from 'Fighting Fifth' Co. Dublin — Frank Lawless, Tomás Ash, J. Peppard, and Jim Lawless. 6 from Louth Batt: Seán McIntee, M[c]Mahon, Jim Sally, F. Martyn, M. Reynolds, M. Quinn: From Cork: D. Kent, Diarmuid Lynch, Con Donovan, Fergus O'Connor. Dublin City: Harry Boland, Gerrard Crofts. From Northern Ireland: Peter Galligan, M. Brady, George Irwin. From London: Frank Drennan, Thornton: & Christy Poole. Partridge and Joyce of Citizen Army. (Poole was brother of Joe the Invincible and was like O'Donovan Rossa, refractory, hunger striking etc.)[18]

Edee was Governor. He wore a huge waxed moustache, and when Tom Stone with sword in hand marched up front, it was hard to suppress a smile. Mr Clarke was chief warder. A quiet decent man. He died suddenly and he was replaced by the very officious Tom Stone but as Stone knew but very little of the bag-making work Mr Geraghty was placed in charge of this department. Bob Brennan worked with him, giving out the material & taking back the finished article. Harry Boland worked at a sewing machine whilst Gerrard Crofts put on the finishing loops. Mr Geraghty was of Irish descent, had a son named Patrick, was editor of the Prison Gazette, and gave any important item of news to Bob Brennan, & as each prisoner had to go to Bob Brennan for and with the material & then with his bag, Bob whispered the news of the day. Besides Bob Brennan and Gerrard Crofts: The Barbers, Frank Lawless, Mick de Lacy and Joe Burke gave & collected news. Although Stone was most officious and held rustics in contempt, he had his favourites, and seemed enamoured of Harry Boland and lauded Mick de Lacy to the skies as 'a lovely boy', gave much latitude to Gerrard Crofts, and felt highly honoured when these approached him.

Just before Xmas 1916 we received the welcome news that we were being sent to Lewes. I had been working at window beside Fergus O'Connor until Colm O'Geary's sight began to fail and I was asked to change places with Colm. I was sent to the central row beside Jim Lawless, Mr Colman, with Joe Howley behind us. Jim was continually criticising and plotting. Fr Finnegan the prison chaplain, who although a native of Cavan averred that as a naturalized Englishman, he was not Irish and had no sympathy with Sinn Féin went round to the prisoners asking them to give an undertaking that they would not try to escape, in return for which the British Government would provide them with civilian clothes and would not send them to Lewes in chains. Jim Lawless began to organize against this. I managed to speak to Brian Molloy, Mick Higgins & Jonny Corcoran, and all the Galway men stood solid as they were IRB men. Seán Etchingham declared, 'We want to appear in public the same as we are treated in private.' Little Joyce's reply was 'I was undecided until you came along, but now I'll go in chains.' And in chains we went. Our gang of nineteen men were in three chains, 7, 7 & 5, each pair was handcuffed together, a chain was then passed between them and locked with padlock to each handcuff; with an odd man in end of each chain. When drawn up at a station every second man ducked under the chain so that a straight line was formed. MacPherson, a Scot was our chief warder. He was friendly and gave us newspapers. As we drew up at Salisbury Station, the soldiers hissed and booed in a threatening manner. The chief warder reproved them telling them they were low cowards to interfere with men in chains, and asserted that if he had to loose their chains these prisoners would make short work of them. The curtains were then drawn until the train proceeded. Old Mich[ae]l Fleming was handcuffed to me. On arrival at Lewes Station a number of excited women collected and one woman shouted 'See the way the brutes have these poor men chained like wild beasts.' In striking contrast to Dartmoor, there was an air of cheerfulness alround. Xmas was coming. The air was pure and wholesome. The Governor, Major Maryat [*Marriott*] was sympathetic, so also the chaplain Dr McLaughlin, who came with the Portland Prisoners, as also Bayley the chief warder. We got tea. It was my first perhaps since my 1st week in Limerick jail, Easter week. The cells were of the usual size but with tiled floors. The work was sewing mail bags, or making door mats, or rugs. We were allowed to speak and to march in pairs at exercise. The popular Welsh warders of Dartmoor, Ayliff and James, came to Lewes, but the officious Chief Warder Tom Stone succeeded in coming also.

The 60 Portland prisoners included Frank Fahy, Scully, George and Jack Plunkett, Connor McGinley, J. J. Walsh, William and Philip Cosgrove [*recte* Cosgrave], Denny Callaghan, Pierce Beasley, Harry O'Hanrahan, Joe McGuinness, J. Burke, Tomás Breathnach etc.[19]

Soon after our arrival at Lewes, George Plunket & Austin Stack asked me to do Keating's Stories[20] with them as Mr Stack who was then a solicitor's clerk in Tralee was studying for an exam. Austin Stack later said he and de Valera were considering the possibility of holding Gaelic classes during exercise. Each instructor to teach 3 others. The snag was, the prisoners exercised in pairs. I suggested that if we did march in fours, the warders may not interfere. We tried it and succeeded. Lewes Prison was transformed into a Gaelic school. I had a class consisting of Colm O'Geary, Connor McGinley and Tomás Breathnach studying Keating's songs, Rannugheacht mór & beag, Deibhi Séadhna, and Caoinc[e]. Eoin McNeill had an old Irish class, & de Valera who organized these classes, had teachers for each grade from beginners upwards. The learners or pupils were taught every second day; the odd days being spent studying what they were taught the previous days. Thus Lewes prison was converted into a Gaelic college. De Valera's scheme was opposed by J. J. Walsh[21] who busied himself in organizing German classes. J. J. succeeded in harnessing two others & himself whilst de Valera mustered all the others for the Irish classes.

Colm O'Geary & myself were appointed to organize the Fáinne and in a short time we had over 30 Irish speakers; each one who made the grade had a button with the tri colours sewn to his jacket. When the Librarian asked me why I sent home for Keating's songs & poems as they had Geoffrey Keating's poems (in English) in the Library, I felt glad to be able to inform him that they could not be effectively translated into English as the Irish Language was more than twice as rich in sound as English, and that it was the skilful weaving of those sounds, in accordance with defined rules for the various types of songs & poems, and not the subject matter which mattered most.

In the Deibhi 'Mór an trom Inis Banba', there is the verse

> 'Mór dhúinn tré ár neamh-ádh anois
> Dhá mhac feardha Mhic Phearais:
> A mórbha tré báidh Banbha
> D'agair an áil a thardha.'
>
> 'Great, to us through our misfortune now.
> The two manly sons of Pearse:
> Their murder through their love for Ireland
> To the tribulation of the Gaelic Patrimony.'

Recently when an Irish scholar was criticising and reviewing Keating's Poems through Radio Éireann, he quoted this verse and said he was surprised that any Irish Scholar did not discover this portentous verse. Not only did it appear in the deibhi itself but it was also given in the Reamhrá as an example of the deibhi form of Irish poetry.

I myself took it to McNeill, and asked him if he had seen it already. He said he had not. Then I asked him what he thought of it. He replied that it was remarkable.

So keen were the students of Gaelic in Lewes Prison, that those working at sewing bags had their Irish books covered with strips of canvas as a disguise.

By this time Indian meal bread was substituted for wheaten bread. The prisoners did not mind, as when fresh this bread was quite as palatable & perhaps as nutritious as the wheaten.

Encouraged by the success of the Irish Language classes, the prisoners decided to launch a manuscript journal in Gaelic and English.[22] It was to contain articles stories songs etc from the prisoners. I was appointed editor. The writers included de Valera, Colm O'Geary, Frank Fahy, Tomás Aghas, Harry Boland, J. J. Walsh, Con Collins, Connor McGinley, J. J. Burke, George Plunket, A. Stack and several others. It was illustrated by Peadar Doyle and McMahon, and myself wrote the leading article. The journal was a tremendous success and was handed round to the prisoners. It was extolled by all and was said to be the first prison journal ever issued We were collecting material for the second journal when the crisis came.

The food ration was reduced to half. The prisoners countered that by declaring a no work strike. The fat was now in the fire. The officious Tom Stone's hawk eye came, and saw how things stood. He thought he had a soft mark in Brian Molloy whose job was mending shoes & whose jersey was twice too big for him. 'Molloy,' he said 'get back to your work.' Brian Molloy showed him his jersey and his answer was 'Arra who could work on that kind of a bella' (belly). The outcome of the strike was that the prisoners were taken back to their cells and kept in solitary confinement. The weather was very warm & the prisoners complained of the stuffy cells. De Valera sent an order to each prisoner to be ready to break his window at 8 o'clock on a certain evening. One or two panes were to be left unbroken to show that it was not out for destruction the prisoners were, but in order to allow themselves fresh air. I was asked to destroy 'treasonable' articles before the journal was seized. I destroyed 3 wild articles written by Harry Boland, Tomás Aghas and J. J. Walsh. De Valera was displeased when his article was not destroyed also. I tore up the 3 wild articles and threw the pieces into a bucket of water before my cell was raided & the journal seized.

We could have been confined for a fortnight before being separated. Lack of exercise left us poor walkers when we were manacled and chained. I was with a number of Galwaymen with Tom Stone and Gallops in command. Drawn up at a railway station we began to whistle 'The wearin of the Green' when the chief warder Stone said 'Dont make your case any worse than it is. Ye conducted yourselves for 6 months, but when we became lenient, ye thought we were fools, and it was against my advice ye got those concessions, but we all looked upon the Sinn Féin prisoners as a superior type of criminals.'

Gallops, probably Welsh, and an adept at learning Gaelic said 'I would consider it a wonderful move had ye succeeded, but I'm afraid your case has been worsened.'

Maidstone

Maidstone, a prison for second-class misdemeanors, is in Kentshire. It has sheetiron cells with a strip of canvas across an angle up in the wall, held in position by two iron crooks. Under the influence of a June sun it was well-nigh unbearably hot. The Sinn Féin prisoners were ordered to the Tinker's shop, or printer's shop. We claimed to be prisoners of war and refused to work. We got three days bread and water, then two days respite and then three days bread & water again & so forth. The chaplain was south English and the colour of the chalk country. He said quietly to me 'They will not recognize ye as prisoners of war. They would rather release ye than that.' This seemed the darkest hour of our imprisonment, but the darkest hour proved to be that before the dawn.

One day I was taken to the Tailor's shop and my measure taken. When I reached my cell I heard a criminal say, 'His measure is taken. They will be released.' We were cautioned not to incite the other prisoners, and were taken by train to Pentonville Taken to a hall we were scrutinized by detectives and warders. On Sunday when de Valera demanded to be allowed to go to mass, the official asked if he would give an undertaking that he would not create a scene. De Valera said he would and would answer also for the other prisoners. Then the chaplain Fr Clery said, 'Look here, these are none of your criminals. These men are fighting for an ideal, and I could give this undertaking for them myself.' The chaplain was a young man and an Irish enthusiast and recited the rosary the prayers and acts in Gaelic. After mass and a meal we were given each a new suit of clothes. The officials became more sociable, and showed us Casement's grave,[23] and the cell occupied by Arthur Lynch[24] when under Sentence of Death.

From Pentonville [we] were taken by train to the port and there we boarded a boat bound for Ireland. Harry Boland gave 'M'anam a Dhía, but there it is.' 'The Soldier's Song' was also sung, and a large crowd awaited the arrival of the prisoners at Dunleary. But this was nothing to the wild scenes at Westland Row,[25] and later in Dublin City itself. Sinn Féin had won a glorious victory and the chains of English Imperialism were being broken.

The Clare Election

Willie Redmond MP the quandom militia captain having joined up was sent to France.[26] He had issued pamphlets appealing to the young men of Ireland to follow him and aid him in the fight for their Religion and the Freedom of Small Nations. He was killed and this brought about the famous East Clare Election. The recently released prisoners & internees were asked to assist. De Valera was chosen as Sinn Féin candidate whilst the Irish Party candidate was Paddy Lynch KC.[27]

I went to Tubber and called on my cousin Frank Brew who harnessed a big clydesdale to a side-car & with Peter Slattery, Mr Dowling & Mr Noonan & a large tri-colour flag we set out for Ennis. At a gateway were some kilted soldiers and a number of women. The latter began making balls of sand & mud & as we came along we were subjected to a heavy volley of mud & sand from those frenzied women. This horse took fright and galloped off. Peter Slattery's glasses, eyes, and ears were daubed with mud, the flag also & Mr Noonan presented a sorry picture. Mr Dowling & myself who were on the far side of the car & Frank Brew on the 'dicky' were only 'slightly wounded'. These were the separation women who attacked us. The separation allowances & drink had transformed these women into Furies. In Ennis a large crowd of these half-maniacs were held back by a force of the RIC. I was put in charge of a body of Volunteers at Crusheen polling booth. In striking contrast to their women folk, the soldiers home on furlough proudly wore the Sinn Féin emblem and voted openly for Sinn Féin.

On the day of the count at Ennis a large crowd led by a Shoemaker adopted a threatening attitude, whereupon they were charged by the Volunteers commanded by Comdt Mick Brennan who swept them off the streets.[28] De Valera's glorious victory in Clare meant the beginning of the end for the Irish Parliamentary Party.

I taught at Toormakeady Irish College the usual six weeks with 5 or 6 other olla[i]mh under the Ard-ollamh Pádraig O'Donnellan.[29] I re-organized Irish classes & taught 7 nights a week. The new classes included Closetoken, Kinvara & Maree. Where schoolhouses were not available, we held the classes from house to house & built halls later in Killeeneen & Closetoken.

Between Irish classes, Volunteers & IRB I was kept fairly busy. In 1918 the Volunteers had been re-organized & the name IRA was the appellation. In 1919 I was appointed Republican Loan organizer for South & East Galway & Colm O'Geary for Connemara.[30] Whilst engaged in this work I visited Mountbellew. I read the name Pádraig Ó Fathaigh over a shop door. The owner was a publican & tailor whilst his sister Mrs Owens was in charge of the catering. This man was a staunch supporter of the Irish Party & sec[retary] of local Branch. Believing the RIC would get confused by the names, I booked there. I held meetings at night in Mountbellew & also visited key men in Menlough, Fohanagh

& other districts. One Sunday there was an important Football match in Athenry & under cover of this [I] cycled to Athenry. I met those I wanted to see & cycled back to Mountbellew.

On Monday, hearing a commotion downstairs, I took the papers and documents I worked on & put them behind a large picture that hung on the wall. Just then a sergeant & policeman entered my room. They wanted to know my name and business. I answered by asking them in Irish what were their names & business. Not understanding Irish they became very angry and rebuked the owner of the house & his sister for keeping a person whose name or business they did not know. I was placed under arrest & passing a shop two men who attended my meetings saluted. Conveyed to the Barracks I was brought before Head-Constable Cassidy a very irritable man. When they could not tell even my name, he became very angry. When I answered his questions in Irish, He said 'I do not understand Irish.' I said 'Ní orm atá an locht.' ['That's not my fault.'] After some more of this kind of questioning & answering, He said 'I'll put you in the lock-up until you talk English.' I said 'Níl ceart agat é sin a dhéunamh mar ní admhuighim an Riagaltas Sasanach agus ní labharfaidh mé leat ach Gaedhilge amháin.' ['You have no right to do that because I do not acknowledge English law and I will not speak anything but Irish with you.']

Before being put in the "black hole" I was searched, and my IRA note book and an envelope addressed to me was found in my possession. The note book contained the number of IRA men in each district, number of arms etc. The number of RIC Barracks, number of RIC arms etc. The name of the club was in Gaelic. The details were in Gaelic also but in shorthand. A shorthand expert Const. Kelly was called in to decipher the shorthand. He blundered badly, taking it for granted that the shorthand notes were English, and as FitzHenry's Gaelic Shorthand is somewhat similar to Pitmans he messed them up.[31] Of *Shee weera* police, he made She Widows. A hot argument ensued amongst the RIC. When asked to explain this, he said it meant that these were the number of widow women as distinct from widowers. The officer told him that was ridiculous, but the expert maintained that 'she widows' was the word.

An ex-soldier was brought in also. He said 'Ye have him now & hold on to him.' From the black hole I could hear what was said outside. The hotel owner Pádraig Ó Fathaigh brought me food and questioned me in Irish. He said I must be a suspicious character & the Peelers to be after me. I brought his questioning to an end by informing him that I did not want to see anyone and was not there to answer questions.

It happened that an RIC official, a head-constable I think, was shot in Tipperary. 'A Sligo Catholic' wrote condemning the murder of Policemen shot down in discharge of their duty, and condemning the instigators who go about organizing. Fr Malachy Brennan replied, condemning the English Government for arresting & detaining Irishmen without trial or charge, merely because they spoke Irish & instanced my case.[32] 'A Mayo Catholic' replied eulogizing the sentiments of 'the Sligo Catholic' & expressing his indignation that [a] noble police officer should be compared to an obscure petty politician name[d] Pádraig Ó Fathaigh. Fr Malachy Brennan again replied and gave a better scorching to the 'Mayo Catholic' than he did to the 'Sligo Catholic'. The 'Sligo Catholic' & 'Mayo Catholic' were believed to be Head-Constables who adopted the tyrant's 'Holy Plan' as a mask for their tyranny. It was the RIC Head-Constables who were in charge of the Secret Service.

On Saturday evening I was brought before DI Scully.[33] He asked me my name & when I answered him in Irish he said he did not know Irish. I said 'Ní orm atá an locht. That's not my fault.' Then he wrote in English 'What is your name?' I wrote in Irish 'Pádraig Ó Fathaigh is ainm dom.' He wrote 'Why don't you speak English?' I wrote 'Is Éireannach mé agus sí an Gaedhilge teanga na h-Éireann. Because I'm an Irishman and Irish is the language of Ireland.' Again he wrote and again I wrote in Gaelic. He smiled good-humouredly and said 'I will let you go.' The members of the Mountbellew IRA were jubilant, and next day being Sunday, they tried hard to bring me with them to the sports. Instead I cycled to Loughrea to meet keymen there & arrived late that evening. I met a man who said, 'You have made praishach of our propaganda by turning up here.' Philip Waldron[34] & other Gaelic Language Leaders held a meeting & delivered violent anti-government speeches & I being there in Loughrea and not dying in the black hole of Mountbellew knocked the pep off their talk & Philip fled from the town. Philip later asked me for an account of the Mountbellew affair which he published in the newspapers.

Whilst organizing the loan I called on Dr Duignan [*recte* Dignam], then PP Duniry.[35] He presided at an after-mass meeting in Abbey. He afterwards informed me that he organized six Gaelic League Branches in the district. He intended employing two Gaelic Teachers, each Branch to have lessons in Gaelic two nights weekly. He applied to the Gaelic League for two teachers, but these could not be supplied. I sent him two of my own pupils who proved very successful. One was Pádraig Kilkelly of Kinvara.[36] I found him digging in a garden. I asked him to accept the job. He flung the spade to the head ridge and came along. Like most Gaelic Leaguers he was an IRA man, and threw himself heart & soul in the national movement. He taught in Abbey, Ballynakill & Woodford I think. He stayed in Abbey and brought Willie Hynes, Kinvara, to assist him.[37] Both were arrested in Spring 1920 and were interned in Wormwood Scrubbs.

During the Winter of 1919 the Kinvara IRB were active, and several ambushes were planned, but the RIC did not turn up on those days It was also planned to attack Kinvara Barracks, and Pat Loughnane[38] and some Beaghe IRB men came to assist, but the RIC patrol who were to be first attacked, came back to Barracks much sooner than usual & thus the attack was frustrated.

After Pádraig Kilkelly and Willie Hynes had been interned, attacks were planned on Kinvara, Kilcolgan and Oranmore Barracks on the same night on Monday. I was acting Comdt for Gort Batt[alion] area at the time. Comdt Seumas Murphy[39] came to Kinvara and said that Kinvara was a difficult problem and postponed the attack on Kinvara until Friday. I went to Galway on Monday to meet the chief Republican Loan Organizer for Connacht. Passing Oranmore, Joe Howley called me, and asked me where I was going and when I would be coming back I told him I had to meet the Rep Loan chief and would return after 10 when the RIC patrols would be gone to their Barracks. He said I must be back before 10, and to have everything seen to for Friday as they would all assist at Kinvara & believed they could easily capture the other Barracks. I was about putting hand-bills and other Loan documents in the speck of my cap as usual, but he insisted in putting them in my cycling stockings.

On the road between Clarinbridge and Kilcolgan I met 4 RIC men in charge of Sergeant Haughy. They were walking two deep. The two in front passed one on each side, when Haughy cried 'Halt'. The men in front gave 'bout turn, and when I got off the bicycle I was between the 4. Haughy searched all my pockets & saddle of bicycle & just when myself and the RIC men thought the danger was passed, he tried my stockings and pulled out bundles of papers. This startled the RIC men so much that the rifles of two of them fell on the road. I was taken to Kilcolgan Barracks. I was left in the day room and Haughy went away. The men were friendly and sympathetic & could not understand why [I would not speak?] or take any food. I knew that the 'eyes and ears of the British Government' were finished. They were all under the influence of drink. The handles were broken off the cups as well as splices here & there They cursed Haughy for not letting me pass & swore they would not let him put me in the Black Hole. Const. Kilmartin said they were watching to arrest me for 3 weeks, and when he as senior constable & another went to arrest me one day, he changed his mind & he said to the other man, 'Pádraig or his bicycle never did anything to me and I'll never do anything to them, and after that you will not speak to me now.' A wild row began between themselves and Constable Toolin attacked Const. Jackie O'Brien with a poker. O'Brien grappled with him and eventually took the poker off him. Sergeant Haughy arrived and lectured the men on their disgraceful conduct. When retiring he ordered Jackie O'Brien saying 'Put him in the lock-up.' 'Alright' said the latter. Then he said to me 'Let Haughy go be-damned. I'm on Sentry duty & you will stay with me and the two of us will have a fine feed.' He felt it very much when I would not take any food. He gave me some bed clothes and I was asleep at day-break when there was a knocking at the door. Const. O'Brien asked who was there. 'Friends' was the answer. 'Friends or enemies, if ye do not clear off I'll put the bayonet in your guts.' 'We are Sgts Anderson & Daly. Let us in. The roads are all blacked & we do not know if any barracks have been attacked or not.' When they gave the pass word he let them in & I jumped out of the bed and when they asked who I was, O'Brien said I was a Gaelic Teacher & they merely took me in when they met me late last night. Even Srgt Haughy was perturbed when I went on Hunger Strike & said it was foolish not to take food. Then the Barracks woman asked me if I would take food sent by Scarry or Hussy & when I refused I was taken to Gort Barracks & placed in the Black Hole where I went on Hunger Strike, and then to Galway jail.

There were a few men from Oranmore for raid on Hangar, one from Spiddle for taking rifle off soldier, five men on suspicion of shooting at Frank Shawe Taylor.[40] The warders were trying to enforce discipline but when some more IRA men arrived from the midlands we felt strong enough to talk, run & jump while at exercise. Mick Martyn, Portumna, was kept in solitary confinement. We decided to go on hunger strike: I was then taken to the Railway Station with an escort of RIC, 2 of them with fixed bayonets The officer in charge produced a revolver which he proceeded to load and then said that if I made any demonstration he would shoot me dead. This was probably because of an incident that occurred at Athenry Railway station when I was being brought from Gort to Galway by train.

Incident at Athenry

When being put on the Galway train at Athenry station three members of the Killeeneen Irish class (Tess Walsh, her brother Paddy & another Killeeneen boy) happened to be pasing by when Tess shouted 'Oh look who they have arrested' and she ran up to the carriage. 'Oh see the way the brutes have his hands tied.' 'Keep her back, keep her back' came the order and the RIC formed a chain with hands and rifles in front of the carriage. 'I'll go in in spite of ye' said the girl as she tried to break through, and after two or three efforts succeeded. The RIC in the carriage tried to push me back, but I too succeeded in reaching the door for a shake hands. As the train began to move, the girl shouted 'Your reign will soon be ended' whilst Paddy Walsh & the other boy hooted the RIC. It was thus a schoolgirl defied the minions of Dublin Castle, but it was this spirit that prevailed in that period.

On arrival in Dublin a company of soldiers was drawn up, and I was marched through Dublin with the RIC in the rere. The RIC was not included in the *Daily Sketch* photograph featuring 'More Sinn Féin Arrests' which appeared next day. On arrival at Mountjoy Jail the escort got Bout Turn, and I with two RIC men were left at the jail gate. A prison official appeared & inquired who the Prisoner was: when informed that it was a Sinn Féiner, the official said we have enough of his sort here. 'Take him out of this.'

I was taken to Ship Street Barracks where a number of soldiers were imprisoned guarded by a Coy of the Leicesters. The prisoners seemed happy, two of them were running a race on their hands when I arrived and all welcomed the Sinn Féin prisoner, and when the RIC escort began peering in through the window the prisoners jeered them, shouting 'Join the RIC and see the other world' until the RIC slunk away. When food arrived the prisoners gave me the best and then kicked up a row with the English soldiers complaining about the food. Two of the prisoners, Cassidy and Keogh, asked me if there was a serious charge against me they would plan an escape. A north of Ireland man later showed me the two English soldiers on guard: 'see their poor physiche [*physique*] and thin necks'. He said if there was a serious charge against me, we could strangle these and escape. Cassidy & Keogh called me aside, and told me he was half mad and not to heed him. Keogh gave me his home address and said he had a large quantity of ammunition & some arms, and if I was released before him I could obtain these. An army sergeant called & asked me to go with him, that my wife called to see me. When I told him I was unmarried he said to come with him anyway but I refused. The prisoners were each supplied with one rug and we had to sleep on the bare floor The place was literally crawling with vermin. One night an English corporal was brought in battered bruised and drunk. He complained that he was kicked and beaten by a number of men. Next morning he complained about the food whilst an old Sinn Féiner got the best of everything. He was told that Sinn Féiners deserved to get the best of everything.

Wormwood Scrubs

One day an English army officer (Lt Wedgewood) asked for me. He then said to a soldier who was with him, 'He doesn't seem to be the desperado I expected.' He then showed me his revolver & counted the bullets as he proceeded to load it. Then he said to me, 'If you try to escape or make the slightest demonstration you will get these.' Lt Wedgewood was a tall youngish officer and looked the snob and the upstart that he was. Outside the Barracks we were joined by a huge DMP [Dublin Metropolitan Police constable]. On the way to the boat we met a stately old woman who said 'Go mbeannuighidh Dia dhuit.' I answered 'Dia's Mhuire dhuith' whereupon the Lt shouted 'Hit him in the head with the rifle.' The Cameron whose name was Smyth whispered to me 'Do not speak for God's sake.' When we reached the boat the DMP had disappeared to the annoyance of the officer. Lt Wedgewood began to boast of how an officer approached when a number of Reserves were drilling and enquired if any would volunteer for the Front. How his comrades smiled scornfully when he stood out. How he killed a German and took the revolver off him. He stressed how brutal the Germans were and how chivalrous the English. I reminded him of his type of chivalry when he gave an order to hit a handcuffed prisoner on the head. 'Do you know what Englishman's god is?' he asked. I said 'I do, the almighty pound sterling.' 'No' he said 'it is his honour, and when yourself and the old lady spoke a language I did not understand, how did I know but it was a plan of escape and I would be dishonoured if I did not carry out my job.' I said if the Germans were brutal, were not the English Anglo-Saxons & therefore Tuetons [*sic*]. He said that it was only the Prussians who were brutal, and the English came from Saxony in Southern Germany. I said the Saxons of Southern Germany were highly civilized as he said, but the English came from Prussian Saxony. He then said that the English were not Tuetons or

Saxons but Celts, and as the majority of the Celts were in the larger island the Celts of Ireland should be ruled by the majority rule. I said if he was a Celt did he know Irish. He said they belonged to the other family of Celts, the Britons or Welsh & he could speak that Language. Right in front of us was a large picture of a Welsh beuty spot, with the name Penn Maen Mawr. Of course he could not. The Cameron asked me could I. I replied that it was ceann cloiche móire in Gaelic, or the head of the big stone in English. I reminded him also that there did not seem to be anything Celtic in the name Wedgewood. 'I see you have my name. I suppose I will be in the Sinn Féin black list, but I do not give two hoots whether or no.' I told him Sinn Féin's quarrel was with the English Government and not with their tools.

Arriving in England at a Station there, a number of women collected & cast angry looks at the escort. The Cameron said 'Why do not these women mind their own business?' I asked why he was not in kilts. He said the Camerons were nearly all slaughtered and said the remnants of 4 regiments were amalgamated into one regiment

Wormwood Scrubbs

On arrival at Wormwood Scrubs, a warder came smiling and said 'You will have fine times here. I'll bring you now to a great friend of yours.' It was James. James who was Welsh had the greatest welcome for me, and said that [in] every prison [where he] himself was warder that I was there also & complimented me. 'After all you went through' he said 'you are here again better than ever.' He brought me to chief warder Bailey who was in Lewes. They informed me that I'd meet some of my old comrades including Jim Lawless who was in Dartmoor and Willie Cosgrove [*recte* Cosgrave] & Harry O'Hanrahan who were in Lewes They were glad to inform me that the Sinn Féin prisoners would get the best of treatment & could play football, handball etc. In contrast to the dark, dreary dismal Dartmoor, everything in Wormwood Scrubbs had a bright cheery look. The food was good & plentiful & luxuries could be bought. The warders were like servants. They polished the prisoners boots. When at church, cushions were placed under their knees It was as if the Government meant to kill Sinn Féin with kindness

I met Martin Finnerty of Gurteen for the first time.[41] I expected to meet a politician of the Jonny Redmond[42] school of thought but instead Martin was a product of the Gaelic League and loved reading Irish stories, and tracing the meaning of place names, local history etc. Then I met Wedger Maher the famous Toomyvara hurler. There were 6 other Toomyvara hurlers in Wormwood Scrubbs, 3 Hartys and 3 Hacketts. Wedger asked me to do *Séadna* with him. We did it thoroughly, 1st the story itself & the meaning of the difficult words, then the nouns & their declensions, and the verbs & their tenses etc according to Mícheál Breathnach's method.[43] When not studying *Séadna* he discussed hurling. He said that the Galway hurlers if properly trained were unsurpassed, & if he had them he would only train the forwards. The backs would do alright but the forwards should be trained. He said Tynagh had enough 1st class hurlers to form the nucleus of a great county team.

Notwithstanding the kind treatment, Wedger Maher like most of the prisoners suffered from 'doleful inaction' and longed to get back to the hillsides. Most of the prisoners demanded release, otherwise they would go on hunger strike. A number of Irishmen & women used come outside the prison & this day at a given signal we broke the jail doors. This was done by insert[ing] a small prayer book or the four gospel[s] between door and jamb, then running & throwing yourself against the door. After my 1st attempt the door gave way a little, then inserting the four gospels further, there was much better results; then doubling the little book I charged with all my strength and the massive jail door was on the floor. In a few moments every Sinn Féiner had his cell door pulled down. An army deserter known as Tommy Atkins ran along the top of stairs and giving a gigantic leap reached a window on the flight underneath & smashed the window whilst the Irish outside the Prison cheered wildly. In the midst of wild excitement the prisoners smashed everything breakable they could lay hold of whilst the warders were powerless. The destruction continued until the Coldstream guards came along with fixed bayonets. Every man was ordered back to his cell, which order was obeyed.

Placed in solitary confinement the bulk of the prisoners began a hunger strike. Jim Lawless who was a member of the committee, disagreed with this and for a few days a minority group partook of food, and then joined in the strike.

Of course the attitude of the warders changed when Larry Lardner asked a warder for water. The warder's reply was 'You will get no water.' 'We will be all dead in six days' said Larry to a group of us standing by. Seeing James standing near I approached him and asked could we get water. 'Certainly' he said 'you can get all the water you care to drink either hot or cold.'

The hunger strike went [on], the prisoners growing colder & feebler from day to day. Two Clare ex-army men were the 1st to collapse, but this could be feigned to test its effects on the officials who were perturbed by hunger strikes. We had a visit from a lawyer, who was brother (I think) of Sir Anthony MacDonnel.[44] He encouraged the prisoners to continue. He said to myself 'Ye have made a wonderful fight & ye will win.' It was stated that Short said he would not let anyone die.[45] The prisoners were examined by a doctor each day and anyone in danger was taken to hospital. I had been 14 days on hunger strike when I was taken to Marleybone Infirmary.[46] A large number of prisoners were here but the prisoners were taken to two other hospitals also.

The nurses in Marleybone (amongst whom were several Irish girls) were very friendly. 1st we got a bath, then hot milk every four hours, and after a few days we were given fried haddock. Then we had visitors. A visiting justice, a Mr Walshe from Co. Mayo, and a candidate for William O'Brien's All for Ireland League, in Co. Mayo, came to chat with me often.[47] He was a tall bearded man. He had a daughter a nurse in Marleybone, and his son passed a difficult exam & got very high marks in Gaelic. A German lady who was a French Teacher brought me French lesson books. Everything seemed to be going alright until Lloyd George was questioned about the Wormwood Scrubbs prisoners.[48] He replied, that when these prisoners were sufficiently recovered they would be taken back to prison. New charts were placed over the Sinn Féiners heads with the words in large letters 'Place of Residence — Wormwood Scrubbs'. This looked ominous. One day a veterinary surgeon Conn Donovan whom I knew in Dartmoor called to see me. He said he came to organize an escape attempt. He said the London Irish had no experience of these things. He said he had drawn up a list of these who could accomodate two or 3 prisoners. That these would come to the Infirmary as visitors. The prisoners for their part would choose any name they might fancy. About 40 of the prisoners in Marleybone were Corkmen. I chose the name Hovenden & a Limerickman said he'd go with me. As the large crowd of visitors were leaving, the prisoners left with them and scattering here and there were soon swallowed up in the London crowds. Mr Hovenden was a tailor and his wife was a manicurist. She was German. His people were originally Dutch & coming over with William of Orange they settled down in Leix, but I think he was London born; his nephew Mr Dowling was arrested at Crabbe Island and he was imprisoned for 'The German Plot'.[49]

Mr Hovenden took us into the Lachmere Hotel. And as we staggered in, the manageress, a tall red-haired woman began to abuse us, saying we were all day at other places & came to her under the influence of drink. She ordered the attendants not to serve us, but going further along the counter we had our drinks almost taken when she bore done again on us. 'Leave this house please, I should have said sir.' & we left hastily as the chucker-out approached. Her accents told us she was Irish and her actions that she was drunk.

We went with Mr Hovenden to his house in Battersea. Mrs Hovenden had Sinn Féin sympathies, as also two schoolgirls who came in, Miss Hovenden a girl with a mass of auburn hair and a small dark-haired Italian. They told us that both refused to sing or stand up at the singing of 'God Save the King' at school Next morning I went to Battersea Park & after a few strolls around slipped off to the bus stop at Lachmere and took a bus to Hyde Park corner. I wandered through the Park where orators and preachers [were speaking], the latter being questioned occasionally by long-bearded Jews. A Miss O'Donnell from Kerry whose brother was with us in the hunger strike recognized me and introduced me to a number of Irishmen and girls who met at this corner under the guise of listening to the preachers. From Battersea I went there everyday, meeting with Gaelic Leaguers and Sinn Féiners. I was introduced to a Mr Roche a Waterford ex-soldier, and Sydney Lucas an Englishman; both gave me their London addresses and both were engaged in the work of getting arms for the Sinn Féiners in Ireland. I had an invitation to a Gaelic League Céilidhe but on that date a meeting of the escaped prisoners was held and the prisoners were advised to leave for Ireland immediately. My newly-made friends were disappointed at this sudden departure as they had not sufficient time to get arms for the Galway IRA. Sydney Lucas had a quantity of arms and ammunitions for the Offaly IRA, and travelled with me in the boat. As the train was approaching Tullamore, he threw the parcels out the window. Himself came off the train at Tullamore & would recover the arms later & deliver them to a Mr Delaney.

With the exception of the Marleybone patients none of the prisoners in the other hospitals made any attempt to escape Arriving in Dublin I met George and Jack Plunkett and they took me to their home where I remained during the night. I also met Peadar Clancy[50] who gave me 500 rounds of Rifle ammunition.

The Black and Tans

The British Government were about to negotiate with Sinn Féin, when the resolution known as the Haverty Resolution was passed: this was manoeuvered by the Castle Agents in Galway City and the few members present fell into the trap. & although there was not a quorum present, this resolution was widely circulated and Lloyd George was induced to send over the auxiliaries to terrorise the rest of Ireland as the Galway white feather resolution was used to show that Turbulent Galway had been tamed. Pádraig Kilkelly who was chairman of Gort District Council & therefore a member of the County Council asked me to draw up a statement which he could send to the Press denouncing the resolution

& pointing out that the great majority of the Co. Council were marked me[n] and could not attend the Council meetings; other members also condemned the resolution, but the Black & Tans were here.[51]

I was staying at my sister's house at Carrowkilleen 3 miles from Kinvara by road but one across the rocks. The Kinvara Coy tried several ambushes but the RIC did not happen to come to Kinvara on those days. I was in touch with two RIC men, one in Kilcolgan & the other in Ardrahan. The Constable in Kilcolgan, Const. D—, knew everything that went on. The Head-Constables were in charge of the Secret Service & as he was employed by some of these to decode the code messages and to draft the reports, he was able to give a description of every enemy RIC . . . place of birth, height, colour of hair & eyes, length of service & his activities. The RIC man in Ardrahan managed to send word of intended raids on a few occasions. Sergt O'C— of Kinvara was a quiet inoffensive type of RIC but Constables Red S—, M, and D— were evilly disposed. On Novembers Day 1920 I went to the house of Patsy Hynes, Dungory where I used to hold Irish classes. Pádraig Kilkelly met me there & with Mikie Hynes and Willie were walking towards Kinvara when Patsy Hynes' brother, Tomás a Gaelic Teacher came running towards us with word that the Black and Tans were in Kinvara. Later we learned that Mrs Quinn nee Eileen Gilligan a former member of Ardrahan Gaelic League and Dramatic Club & wife of Malachy Quinn the famous Kiltartan hurler had been shot dead at her own gate whilst holding her child in her arms and a Peterswell small farmer had been robbed of £80 by crown forces.[52] I was advised not to stay at my sister's house at night but as I had a very sore knee from boils I chanced staying there for some time until Mich[ae]l Nilan invited me to stay at his house, which I did until with the Kilkelly & Hynes we set up two tents in the hazel cover between Carrowkilleen & Killanaill. One of our number slipped into Kinvara every morning & night. We could muster 8 Kinvara men at short notice & 3 or 4 members of the mid-Clare Brigade came often to assist. The RIC did not turn up the day of the ambush, but next day perhaps the very active Sergt H. marched to Kinvara with a dozen RIC. The Crown forces were raiding

& burning & in addition to the RIC there was a force of Auxiliaries in Drumharsna Castle nearby. Several houses in Ardrahan Peterswell and Kinvara were burned down. I had a message from Sydney Lucas saying that a number of London Irish were willing to come to our district to form a flying column, but the local Comdt replied that [it] was arms we wanted not men. I then got in touch with Liam Mellows & asked him to form a flying column but he was not available, then I sent a request to Tomás Malone, but he had been captured.[53] Then we chose Pádraig Kilkelly. He selected the Foy's House a one-time hospital, and sent for the IRA men of Ardrahan & Kilmacduagh & Ballinderreen who were then on the run to form his flying column. He sent me to Carran Co. Clare for some arms, & when I returned I met some Kinvara IRA & Tom Gibbons of Ballinderreen, who informed me that when the Ardrahan & Kilmacduagh men saw the situation of Foy's House, they said it was a death trap and refused to stay there.

Four of us Pádraig Kilkelly, Willie Hynes Tom Gibbons & myself were at Patsy Hynes & 4 or 5 others were at Hamberry's [*Hanbury's*] house. The guns were hidden away when four RIC men came along and began firing at seagulls. Gibbons said, 'Have we 4 revolvers?' & on being informed that there was, he said, 'Then let the 3 of ye come with me & we'll each take a man.' We were just as far as the road when a Crossley Tender of Auxiliaries came along, and pulled up near Hanbury's. Mikee Hynes dashed out of Hanbury's to warn us, and although the Auxiliaries fired on him he was uninjured & the 5 of us crossed the fields. Joe Kilkelly, Séumas Davenport & one or two others who were at Hambury's came under fire as we did, but the day was very rough & no one was hit although Joe Kilkelly lay down from exhaustion. When the auxiliaries returned they later burned Hambury's cock of straw & as Hyne[s]'s house had already been burned, they threatened to burn Hambury's whereupon Const. McD[ermott] our friend & another Const. who was unpopular levelled their rifles and swore they would shoot any Tan who would approach the house.

In hand to hand struggle with the local IRA captain outside the Tirneevin church, an ex-RIC sergeant was killed. The ex-sergeants son an auxiliary captain came home & went round with a hurley in his hand with the intention of killing the IRA captain with a hurley as his father had been killed. Hearing about this, Pat Loughnane the Beaghe capt. asked his lieutenant Palkey Neilan to accompany him to meet the Auxiliary capt. As the Black & Tan came along on his usual stroll Palkey Neilan jumped on him & held his hands whilst Pat Loughnane took his revolver. They then marched him back to his house and ordered him to yield up all the arms and ammunition which he had. The stuff given up included a sword.

Death of the Loughnane Bros

Fr Nagle PP Shanaglish[54] sent for Pat Loughnane & Palkey Neilan He gave them some cartridges and told them they must go 'on the run' immediately. Palkey tidied up at home — then called for Pat Loughnane but the latter said he could not go until he threshed the corn. While engaged in threshing the place was surrounded by Crown Forces, with Jock Burke in charge of the Tans & Sergt L— whom he hit in Tubber, and Red S as 'pointers'. One of the attendants fled and was fired on, and in the confusion Pat also bolted, but unfortunately turned into the barn where the Tans were in force. Pat and Harry were arrested as also a neighbour.[55] The Loughnanes were taken to Gort RIC Barracks where they were brutally beaten. Jock Burke commandeered a length of rope at Coen's store Gort. The neighbour was released but the Loughnanes were taken away.

Eleven days after the disappearance of the Loughnane Bros a neighbour Micky Loughnane cycled to the spot where Pádraig Kilkelly, Willie Hynes and myself were. He informed us that he had discovered the bodies of the Loughnanes in a pond at Owenbristy as was shown to him in a dream — we immediately set out for Owenbristy. Patsy Hynes got Heleberts float, and when Willie Hynes and another boy had taken the bodies out of the water they were placed on the float hurriedly as the Auxiliaries were in Drumharsna Castle. I was sent ahead scouting and was held up by a stranger who asked me where we were taking the corpses. I said Owenbristy was in Ballinderreen Parish, therefore we had to take them to Ballinderreen Church. The man happened to be an RIC man holidaying with his brother.

When the Tans came in pursuit they headed for Ballinderreen until they found out their mistake at Kilcolgan and afterwards made another mistake. In the meantime the brothers were waked at Hynes' Barn.[56] As the rosary was being recited blood began to flow from their wounds. Dr Connolly[57] who was present said he could give no explanation for this. Pádraig Kilkelly who was in charge asked me to write their names ages & cause of death in Irish which he copied & put on the breast plates. I sent notice of their deaths, the manner of their deathes etc to *The Irish Independent*.[58] Tomás Ó h-Eidhin took photos of their mangled bodies in the[i]r coffins before being taken to Kinvara church. As the coffins were being taken from the church at Kinvara to the hearses one or two lorry loads of Tans drove up to the gate. A passage was made in the centre of the cortege & the 'wanted men' passed back to the rere. After firing shots in the air the Tans drove away We accompanied the cortege through Kinvara until ordered to withdraw.

I had a few narrow escapes. It was Mikie Hynes' day to mind the tents & guns. As I prepared to venture back to my sisters place he asked me to bring him a can of water. The path to the well led through a wood of hazel & giant holli[e]s & was a mile away. It took me probably an hour before I returned and then went for Carrowkilleen. Beside the gate to the long boreen a man stopped me & told me Sgt H— with a force of RIC were just leaving the place. They took the handkerchief with the blood of the Loughnanes and the name Marleybone Infirmary printed thereon. The[y] also took my bicycle as far as the road, but as I took away the chain as a precaution they flung it against the wall. Another day I ventured to Carrowkilleen & after a short stay at the house, I was reading a book near the end of a long boreen where I awaited the arrival of a messenger with information. On lifting my head I saw a large force of RIC coming along the road. I ran back the boreen and then crossed into a field & crawled along beside a wall which ran parallel to the road. I heard voices & one said 'he may come out this way'. While awaiting a message the previous week I ventured out on the road & a Gort car happened to pass. A friend in Gort sent word that I was to be raided for that day, but the messenger who was a neighbour of Pádraig Kilkelly's thought he was the Pádraig in question. Const. MacD sent Miss H— to warn me that Sergt looked to be on for mischief. She came 1st to Carrowkilleen & not finding me there went to our camp where she was roundly abused for coming near the place, as she told my sister when she visited her the second time that day. Indeed far from complimenting me on my escape Pádraig Kilkelly and Willie Hynes upbraided me for my rashness. McD— afterwards told Miss H— that Sergt H— had a force of 14 men but that himself was the only RIC man who saw me.[59]

With the exception of Athenry the people of Kinvara were the most alert in Co. Galway and the IRA were always safe there. We used attend Mass every Sunday & holy day chiefly at the Convent. DI Blake[60] the most active police official that came to this District discovered this. He notified Sergeant Mooney, Gort, & Constable Durcan[61] to meet him at Kilcolgan Barracks. The DI said he had information that 5 wanted men attended mass at Kinvara every Sunday & holy day. These were 2 Hynes, Kilkelly, Davenport & myself. He said he would give them a force of auxiliaries to surround the church. They were to take the 5 to Kilcolgan Barracks without abuse or torture & shoot them immediately. The DI then asked Sgt Mooney which church were they likely to attend. Sgt M— said he did not know, but that Const. Durcan might be able to tell him. Const. Durcan said he wouldn't have an idea, it could be one or the other. The DI said 'It is probably the Parish church. Now there are only 3 of us that know this & I hope nobody else will know of it.' 'No fear' said Sgt Mooney. 'The devil a fear' said Durcan.

Durcan found it difficult to get an opportunity of warning us but he risked his life in sending me a despatch through the lady to whom he gave his messages. We did not go to Mass that Sunday, but Willie Hynes was under the wall when the six Crossley Tenders passed & on the last lorry was chalked 'The last hope'. The Parish chapel was surrounded and as the people came out, the younger men were seized and made lie on the road for the Black and Tans to walk over and jump on. Needless to state the most officious man there was Constable Durcan. Soon after this some IRA men from Mid Clare Brigade asked me to join the Flying Column. They said they asked Pádraig Kilkelly several times and would not ask him again. The Leader said he knew I had a Colt repeating rifle & some revolvers. They took or was given a large quantity of ammunition for the colt rifle. This was obtained from a friendly ex-army officer. I replied that I would go immediately. Pádraig Kilkelly & Willie Hynes overheard or guessed what was afoot & coming up said if I would wait until Sunday they too would join the Mid-Clare flying column.

Willie Hynes had a revolver and I had given one to Pádraig Kilkelly when we set out on foot for the Burren mountains. Kilkelly found it very difficult to tear himself away from his dearly loved Kinvara and like Lot's wife he was continually looking back and lingering so that it took us the whole day to reach Carran. We called at Mrs Diffly's & was received with the warmest welcome. Mrs Diffly was a Gaelic enthusiast and taught at a local school whilst her husband was an RIC sergeant serving in the Abbey District of South Galway. Her two sons were ardent Sinn Féiners. Her sister was tried for her Sinn Féin activities and the Comdt of the 5th Active Service Unit was a near relative. After a few days we were summoned to a meeting. It was a very wet night. The meeting was held in a barn full of skutched wheat. There were a great many items on the agenda and each was fully considered. We were told to stay in Carran & await further orders. The men of Carran were a tough & fearless type & fine scouts so that when the Black and Tans raided Mrs Diffley's house no wanted men were there. Debarred from Mrs Diffly's the only safe place was the house of the Parish priest. The housekeeper was sister of a prominent Carran IRA man whilst the clerk 'Trapper' Hehir was an alert vigorous youth. The priest although a brilliant writer was a quiet easygoing old man. The Xmas stations were on which necessitated early bed time for the clergyman & as soon as the latter retired 'Trapper' closed the doors & opened the parlour window. Before retiring, the housekeeper had left supper for the men on the run. Sleeping on the floor of the well-carpeted cosy parlour was a Godsend to the outlaws. After breakfast each morning we stole away again before the arrival of the priest & Trapper. The food, cakes etc were given to the housekeeper as 'presents to the PP' who was unaware of our nocturnal visits.

Getting an order to join the 5th unit & repair to Tullagh we crossed the fertile Léim an Eich [*angl.* Leamaneh] district & arrived at the hill of Tullagh a couple of miles from Kilfenora. There were three dwelling houses on Tullagh hill which could be seen miles away as the district is very bare. The houses were roofed with huge flags quarried in the district. Comdt Peadar Ó Lochlain's house[62] was but a short distance away, and Carrahan village was also nearby.

Mid Clare Brigade

The Leaders of the Mid-Clare Brigade were Comdts Frank & Joe Barrett of Ennis.[63] There were 5 Battallions with 5 Flying Columns but after the fight between the 5th active service unit with the marines at Ballyvaughan in which 2 marines were killed and several wounded and 8 rifles captured, Ballyvaughan was detached from Kilfenora & formed the 6th Battallion and 6th active service unit. There were then 6 Battallions and 6 active service units in the Mid-Clare Brigade. Each active service unit consisted of eleven men (all or nearly all marked men) who kept their rifles beside them. After Con Collins had inspected the Brigade he told me it was the best organized in Ireland & was superior to the well-organized Cork Brigades. He said this was largely due to Comdt Frank Barrett.

Pádraig Kilkelly, Willie Hynes & myself were lodged in the three Tullagh houses. I stayed at the house of Paetie [*sic*] & Mrs McCormack. Petie was a travelling salesman for a tea co[mpan]y and their[s] was a large family of young most intelligent & interesting children. After a short time I was sent to Corkscrew to stay with a wounded IRA officer. He was Comdt Seán Macnamara of Ballyvaughan, afterwards Comdt of 6th active service unit.[64] We stayed at the schoolhouse at night & at the teacher's residence in the daytime. The teacher was Miss Lyne of Kerry & relative of Comdt Danny Allman.[65] The wound in hip caused by a ricocheting bullet was fast healing and one day he felt able to cycle on one leg to Kilfenora. A Crossley Tender came along & we had time to get over a moat fence which although slanted on the inside hid us from view. One Sunday as we were about to proceed to Neuchville Church we were warned that military were in the vicinity. The church was surrounded, and 2 men who bolted were fired on several times but happened to escape. Whilst at Corkscrew we read of the Headfort (Kerry) ambush in which Comdt Danny Allman was killed. When the IRA took over the collection of Rates I assisted Seán Macnamara in collecting the Ballyvaughan District.

When Mikie Hynes, Joe Kilkelly and Sunny Purcell arrived the 5th active unit consisted of Comdt Peadar O'Lochlin, his brother Paddy, Joe Kilkelly and Pádraig, Mikie Hynes & Willie, Sunny Purcell, Paddy Ward, Seán O'Callahan, Tommy Collins (now chief supt GS [Garda Síochána]) and myself. Peadar O'Loughlin was Comdt of unit, and I was appointed adjt [adjutant].

The procedure was The active service unit visited a co[mpan]y area The coy was ordered to put up barricades, cut trenches across the roads etc. whilst members of the unit drilled the coy members every evening. The longest stay was a fortnight & before leaving, the unit with the local coy should carry out an ambush or attempt an ambush, & then the unit travelled by night to a distant coy area.

One night the 5th contemplated a surprise attack on an enemy force at Lisdoonvarna, but scouts brought word that the enemy had taken up positions outside the town. Another ambush planned by the Carran men, on the Lisdoonvarna road did not come off as the Black & Tans did not come that way. For a time the unit stayed in a tent which was placed beside a cliff and 'Pat Cahill' ex-army Lt Powell had it camouflagged [*sic*] by painting a fir tree on the canvas. One night as we were engaged in cutting the road in expectation of the Tans, a matchmaking Party coming from Kilfenora with horse and side-car fell into the trap. Some men from the unit assisted in getting the horse & car out. This accident did not thwart the match-making and the unit was invited and attended the wedding.

Having received a message from Comdt Tom Shalloo that the enemy forces attended at church in Ennistimon, Comdt O'Loughlin set out on

Sunday morning. After telling off Tommy Collins for the purpose of taking down the tent about the time of the attack, he had 12 men with himself. Comdt O'Loughlin always marched in front of his men. He was a lithe active six-footer, well educated and fearless, and with his neat uniform and long service rifle was a fine type of Sinn Féin officer. He informed his men that it meant a run of five miles to get clear of the encircling road which could be used by the enemy forces. Near our destination we met Comdt Shalloo and Jimmy Murroughy. The latter took on Sentry duty, whilst Comdt O'Loughlin sent 8 men to attack the enemy coming from church and took 4 others to cover the retreat. I happened to be in the latter group. The 8 men rushed across a paddock and fired on the enemy in the street. Then the 5 kept firing on the Barracks to allow the 8 to get back & to check the pursuit. The enemy guns both machine & rifle soon opened fire, but the 5 kept answering these until the Comdt called it off. Running back we soon saw the 8 men in front of us & at length came up with them. Paddy Ward informed us that a bullet lodged quite close to him. When it was reported that one of the men W.H. was lost, the Comdt said 'If we go looking for him we'll all get lost.' He turned up alright and the 8 men escaped in a boat across Lickeen lake.

The Comdt who had a touch of diabetis got thirsty; we entered a house where a lone man sat at table drinking tea. As we were very hungry we looked for food, but the man had neither food nor drink. There was a large bowl of sugar on the table as well as a large paper bag of the same stuff beside it. Five hungry men soon had gobbled up the bowl of sugar and we took the sugar in the paper away in our pockets.

It was a cross country run. 'We'll chance the road now' said the Comdt and as we reached Cahersherken, Paddy O'Loughlin looked back and said 'The Black & Tans are on us.' We jumped over a moat & took up a bad position on the exposed side of a moat. It happened that we tore up a culvert on the road beside our position the previous night and we could hear the despairing cries of the Black & Tans as their lorry went into the trench. We were about 50 yards from the road & awaited an attack. Then a scout was sent out who informed us that the Tans made for the nearby Cahersherken cottage which they occupied expecting an attack.

Comdt Peadar O'Loughlin was promoted and took up duty at Brigade Headquarters office at Ennis & Pádraig Kilkelly was appointed Comdt of Unit 5th. A force of marines were stationed near Ballyvaughan. Although an enemy force of occupation they were not aggressive. For a while they went about unarmed, but later went about fully armed. Seán Mac of Ballyvaughan decided they should be attacked when passing through Ballyvaughan. Accordingly the 5th active service unit with the local IRA Coy & others entered the town at dawn, seized the Post Office and took up positions in the streets through which the marines would pass. Paddy O'Loughlin, M. Kelliher & myself took possession of a ruined stable & fixed the walls so that we had cover from enemy fire. The [*illegible*] girl was prevented from answering the marines' questions who wanted to know if all was well in Ballyvaughan. After waiting all day a scout brought news that the Black & Tans had left their Barracks, and the line up call was given. The men were then marched through the street and were about to disperse for home when the news came that the marines were approaching. And there was a rush for the vacated position. As our position was in the far end of street, we were ordered to go back as the marines were quite near. Tommy Collins, Joe Kilkelly & myself were about to enter the Post Office when it was closed against any others. We then took up position commanding one of the roads that led to the town. We held our position until the firing died down & no enemy forces either entered or departed by this route. Discovering that what we first took to be an enemy outpost were our own scouts, we crossed some very high walls for the purpose of re-joining our unit. We saw no sign of these, but came under machine gun fire as we retreated. The missiles lodged in a bare limestone ridge beside us and sent fragments of the rocks flying in all directions, but we kept to the level ground & escaped. After a long journey we came to a road and asked a passerby the name of the place. He informed us that some IRA men passed by some time before us. We soon came up with four or five men who were sitting by the roadside.

Comdt T.G. the man in charge informed us that they were from the Lisdooonvarna area, that the enemy losses were two killed & several wounded & that we had captured 8 rifles with bandoliers etc. T.G. said that when he went to get the rifle off a wounded marine, the latter said 'What good will it do you to kill me? Am not I bad enough as I am?' T.G. replied 'We do not want to kill you. We only want the rifle.' One result of the Ballyvaughan fight was, that there were enough rifles for another active service unit. Ballyvaughan was detached from Kilfenora with Comdt Seán Macnamara who planned the attack as Comdt of new unit. This clash could not be described as an ambush as the marines came in extended formation, skirting the houses on both sides of the street, but had they come half an hour sooner when the IRA were posted here & there throughout the street, very few of the 32 marines could have escaped.[66]

Peadar O'Loughlin had taken up duty at Ennis with Brig[ade] Comdt Frank Barrett. The result was the perfection of the organization. The 5th Unit visited each company area in turn. An order came from Headquarters that the Lts of the units should drill the men as well as the Comdt.

Willie Hynes who was promoted Lt was called upon to drill one evening. He asked me to take his place. I lined the men for drill and put them through the movements. The result was I was appointed drill instructor. Since the attack at Ennistimon we discarded the tent & put up [in] the houses. When arriving at a company area, the Comdt asked for five houses where the unit would stay. Comdt Pádraig Kilkelly, Lt Hynes and Paddy O'Loughlin took No 1 & so on unto No 5 which was given to Mikie Hynes & myself. Mikie used smilingly say 'give us the last one'. The company would be mobilized, the men were required to cut & block roads, have scouts and sentries given their special duties & the men would be drilled and trained every evening; before a fortnight had elapsed there would be planned an ambush, but the Tans usually shunned the Coy area until 2 or 3 days after we had left, when they arrived & made the farmers remove the obstacles. Meanwhile having travelled by night, our unit would have taken up duty in a distant Coy area where the usual blocking of roads, drilling etc. would take place.

The unit was received with the greatest welcome everywhere & the spirit of Patriotism & self-sacrifice permeated old and young.

Dysert

About the middle of May 1921 the unit was ordered to repair to a place near Dysert where an attack on the Black & Tans by way of an ambush was planned. More than a hundred men under the command of Comdt Frank Barrett awaited the dawn and a general absolution was given by Canon H.[67]

The night was very wet, and I was asked to go into the house where the officers were. They informed me that an ambush had taken place at Ballytur[i]n which is about 3 miles from my home; that the notorious DI Blake, his woman friend, a Mr Williams, two military officers & an RIC constable were killed. The spot selected for the Dysert ambush was thought to be far too small for the number engaged, but Comdt Barrett ruled that he'd pack them in there, as they were brought there. News came that the Tans left Ennis in 6 lorries. It happened however that a Martini-Enfield rifle was accidentally discharged whereupon the Black and Tans returned to Ennis. No one could be blamed for the discharge of the Martini-Enfield as the least shake was enough to discharge this type of rifle.

It was a great disappointment to the large IRA Force which included riflemen, shotgun men and Bombers. Had this ambush been successful a unit of the Mid-Clare Flying Column would take up duty in South Galway.

DI Blake's Activities

After returning from Dysert to the Kilfenora district I was informed of the death of my sister Mary. During her illness, DI Blake made 13 raids on the house looking for me. He searched under her bed and walked on the bed-clothes. 'If I had to go down to Hell to get him, I'll get him' he declared. She was not afraid, and she knew my brother Mícheál who never knew fear, was seldom far away. One night seeing the Crown Forces enter the house he slipped in with them. After questioning him,

DI Blake whispered to one of the raiders to take him. As he was being taken away Constable Barney Higgins approached and said to the Tans 'I am in charge of this prisoner.' As they both walked in together the constable said 'There is no fear of you while I'm with you; but if I am called away, the Tans will want to bring you out. Say you cannot go anywhere without Barney Higgin[s]'s permission.' When they arrived at Barracks in Galway Constable Higgins was sent for. After the con[stable]s had left a low-sized RIC man approached Mícheál and asked 'Are you a Sinn Féiner?' Mícheál replied 'What is a Sinn Féiner?' The Peeler again demanded 'Are you a Sinn Féiner?' 'If you tell me first what is a Sinn Féiner, I may be able to tell you whether I am or not. Tell me' he said 'what is the meaning of Sinn Féin?'

The Peeler went back to the Black & Tans and said 'He says he is a Sinn Féiner.' Whereupon the auxiliaries pressed him strongly to go out with them. He said he had to wait for Barney Higgins who was in charge of him. When Const. Higgins returned he asked Mícheál if they tried to bring him out. He told the const. that they did & furthermore a low-sized RIC man told the Tans 'He said he was a Sinn Féiner.' 'What I did say' said Mícheál 'was, What is a Sinn Féiner?' Barney smiled 'I knew you'd give a puzzler.' 'Is that the low-sized man you speak of yonder?' On getting a reply in the infirmitive [*sic*], Barney walked to the man in question; on returning he said, 'I have squared him; you are all right now.' After spending some time in Galway jail Mícheál was released.

Mary was the youngest of our family. When two years of age she got the croup and the doctor declared that she would not recover. But my mother gave no credence to him & made no use of the bottle he gave, and Mary did recover, but she was never robust. Since Liam Mellows visited the house in 1915 there had been raid after raid down the years. The 98 Centenary Records, *United Irishmans* and books and pamphlets as well as Liam Mellow[s]'s tent, photos etc.

She took Liam Mellow[s]'s photo from the RIC, telling them they could touch nothing belonging to the house They left the photo back. I succeeded in making one or two visits during her illness in 1915. She was secretary of the Ballycahalan Cumann na mBan whose members carrying banners which they held aloft marched in front of the procession in Athenry in 1915 with Cluad Chevasa at their head.[68]

She died on May 14 1921. When the coffin reached Kilbeacanty it was seized by the RIC and those attending the funeral were chased away by the Crown Forces. It was the same at the funeral; even when a well-known loyalist went to reason with them he was beaten with revolvers.

Meanwhile their chief DI Blake his lady friend & two military officers were feasting at Ballytur[i]n. When the feast was over & when they reached the gate opposite gate lodge as they started for Gort they met the IRA. One lady Mrs Gregory was taken to safety. DI Blake, the lady who was with him and the two military officers all fell, 3 in the car, and one who left the car & put up a fight was killed outside. Crown forces were rushed to the place and one of them Constable Carney[69] was shot dead on arrival. The Auxiliary officers were also doing Secret Service work; Const. Carney used type out these and send copies to the IRA. I heard it said that it was the Tan Ab— who shot him I received some of these SS [secret service] reports as also invitation letters to the DI from Miss Bagot, Mrs Lynch, Mrs Gregory and others. Mrs Gregory's letter seemed to be an answer to something said or written by DI Blake. She told him his methods would never succeed, not in Ireland. 'You say I say these things because I'm a Sinn Féiner. If that is so, I can name numbers of loyalists who have the same opinion as I have Two wrongs do not make a right, and putting down what you call "savagery" with worse savagery will not make things better.' The letters from Miss Bagot & Mrs Lynch eulogized the dinners they had prepared for him; the former declared that she had 'a cake that would go to DI Blake's heart'. This may have enticed the DI to Ballytur[i]n & to his doom.

Note — Mrs Gregory, daughter-in-law to Lady Gregory, afterwards married Captain Gough of Lough Cutra Castle. Her 1st husband Lt Gregory of Air Force was killed in 1st World War.[70]

Burnings

On returning from Mary's funeral,[71] Seán [Ó Fathaigh] said 'Do not attempt to stay here to-night. Take anything ye care about.' Later he called again and said 'Get away from here as quick as ye can. I am leaving this minute.' Mícheál was drowsy and lonely after Mary who was his favourite. My sister Brighid took out a churn & a few other things and then found Mícheál sleeping. She advised him to leave. He at length consented & said, 'Go & stay with Nora Lynskey & I will stay at Pateen Hartes or in the nearby cave at Cromlackagh.' The Crown Forces came like demons. 8 RIC men took up positions behind a moat fence near the house. They set fire to the house and stables and also Seán's house nearby & anything of value that lay near they threw into the fires.

Our next door neighbor Patsy Callinan who was watching so that his own house would not take fire, as he told the burners, was ordered to leave & with his wife & little child unclad had scarcely time to flee when their home was burned down — also the house of Murty Coen.

Clifden

Having received information that the Corofin auxiliaries got water regularly at a place named Clifden ¼ of mile from their headquarters, the 5th Unit retired to Ballyconneely (Co. Clare) and with members of the Coy made preparations for an attack In addition to rifles & shot guns we had a cannon gun also The fortnight was spent in melting lead to make bullets for the can[n]on. On the day of the attempted attack we set out before day as it was necessary that we should have taken up our positions before daylight. The cannon gun was conveyed in a donkey cart. The force consisted of the 5th & 6th active service units with the Ballyconneely Coy; with Comdt Andy Donoghue of the 4th in command.

At some distance from Clifden we called at a village and asked for tea. 6 or 8 men went to each house. There was very wet turf in the house we went to, and the girls were hard set to light it, though they threw in parafin oil and fanned with their aprons. The others in the other houses were ready while we waited on. Pádraig Kilkelly looked in and asked what delayed us, he then went to Andy Donoghue and the latter came in, in a temper & ordered us out immediately. It was a very warm day. The riflemen were placed opposite the pump, the cannon which 8 men carried from the cart was set on its carriage and roped to a tree. Andy Donoghue was to work the cannon. Andy Hayden had charge of the shot gun men who were to lay concealed until the Auxiliaries entered the yard, when they would put wall across road to cut off their retreat. We were to remain until 7 p.m. in expectation of the Tans. Most of the riflemen slept at their posts. There was no sign of the Tans. At 6 o'clock the men of the 6th Unit who had the longest journey said it was time to leave, & the Tans were expected at 3 p.m. A whistle was blown to recall the men and 8 men were bearing the tube of the cannon whilst most of the others were in a cluster going away when the Tans arrived. Seeing how things were, they beat a hasty retreat but their way was barred. They then [*sic*] The auxiliaries began firing & the IRA was ordered to retreat across a green field; about ⅔ of the IRA got across the field: but one third was cut off. Paddy O'Loughlin led these up the face of the cliff. When the IRA returned the fire the enemy firing ceased. It was stated that 3 auxiliaries were wounded, Andy Donoghue was also slightly wounded. The shotgun men crossed under the road by means of a gullet. The 5th were asked to stay in a large gullet under the road that night, but instead they kept moving around. The cannon was recovered by men of the IRA next morning.

Jimmy Murroughy and Kelliher fashioned a dug out from a turf Bank packed with planks & straw and spread turf over it. We had to go down head foremost, then give sharp turn & go down head foremost again. The floor and side-banks were lined with green rushes There was ample space for the eleven men, but it was dark and water oozed from the sides. After a few days, the passage down was widened and after a week, seeing there was no round up by enemy forces, the 5th unit again resumed their usual activities.

After emerging from the dug out we crossed over some fields. We met a number of men at a gateway; one a low-sized stockily-built middle-aged man, smoking a clay pipe was conspicuous. We were apportioned to the houses. Mikie Hynes and I went with the middle-aged man. It was a house in a remote corner, hidden amid a clump of sally trees.

With the exception of Mikie Hynes no one wanted to sleep with me. I was supposed to have elbows and knees like razors, and Joe Kilkelly averred that he lost 3 buckets of sweat the night he was with me. There was one bed for 3 of us and the man of the house chose the central position with Mikie at the wall and I in the brink The poor man was tortured all night & told us so in the morning. The second night the man said we'd never crush him between us again and stayed at the brink and I was in the middle. When I awoke I discovered that I had thrown the man out on the floor à la the young cuckoo. The 3rd night, the man of the house informed us that he was going inside at the wall, with Mikie in the centre. But I mustn't have stayed long at the brink for when I awoke in the morning I saw the man of the house sitting with his back to the wall with his two legs against Mikie's body in an effort to keep him back.

The man had enough of us. The woman of the house said to me that they had men drawing turf and therefore she could not keep us. I said our stay would not interfere with the men as we would only come there at dusk and depart again at dawn. 'Even so I cannot keep ye any longer.' The only other house available was one on the roadside where the Tans sometimes passed. The owner's sons watched for us while we slept and we lay down in an adjoining field during the day as the weather was very fine. But the long fine days aided the Crown forces and one fine morning a party of military crept on with bare feet and captured Comdt Tom Shalloo in the house where he slept. Because of a false alarm the 5th unit as well as the men of the Coy were called out one night. It just showed how these could be mobilized at a moment's notice. Because of a very trivial incident two members of the 5th Unit one a lieutenant were discharged. Friends & neighbours of the officer who discharged them, the three seemed inseparable & the discharged men would do anything for their officer. Andy Hayden & another IRA man were selected to fill the vacancy. We went round the coast by Doolin & Luagh where there was a large Coy of alert men. [It was] at Crab Island near Luagh that Dowling was arrested.

We had been to Moher where we further split the unit 6 & 5. Mikie Hynes & I stayed at Mrs Frawleys. With the exception of the man whom we so nearly crushed to death nothing could exceed the welcome we received wherever we went.

The Truce

It was reported that the Tans frequently passed the Lisdoonvarna road. Our unit took up position at Doon which as its name indicates is a fort. Inside these mounds we lay down after day expecting the Tans We were suddenly recalled and coming to our favourite spot Tullagh, we heard of a Truce. We then went to O'Briens of Lickeen where Seumas Davenport stayed, and the news was true. Comdt Peadar O'Loughlin ordered that all operations would cease at 12 that night. The men of our unit & others decided to go to Kilfenora, but the people of the house said to me not to go as I was not drinking, and, Andy Hayden said the two of us would go to Kilfenora next day.

Next day we heard that 2 Black & Tans had been shot at Doolin the previous day. Andy Hayden called for me as arranged and we both armed with revolvers went to Kilfenora. We met Comdt Peadar O'Loughlin's father and he warmly congratulated us on the turn events had taken. An IRA man Arty Geraghty saluted us from the opposite side & then entered Considine's whilst the three of us went into O'Brien's. We were on the point of departing when I turned back to get sweets. A messenger shouted that the Tans were coming. We had barely time to get over a high moat & lie among the drills of potatoes when the Black & Tans did arrive & in a savage mood. They entered McCormick's shop looking for Sinn Féiners and forced some men they met to tear down Sinn Féin notices. They said they got no order re truce & were in Galway since the previous day. They went there with two of their comrades who were shot down near Doolin. Andy Hayden crept out to the street & returning informed me that the Tans had departed. We again went back to O'Brien's & Arty Geraghty who had lain among the grasscorn waved to us & went back to Considine's. Scarcely were we settled down when the warning came that the Tans were coming back. We again rushed up to the potatoe garden whilst Arty made for the oat field. Later the message came that all was well.

It was a favourite trick of the Tans to double back on the expectation that the IRA would become careless.

The Truce was proclaimed & observed. We had a meeting at Carmody's hotel, Ennis. The men there felt uneasy as it was reported that Ignatius O'Neill[72] & 'Pat Cahill' had been drinking since the Truce with two Auxiliaries and fears were entertained for their safety. That night to our astonishment there arrived Ignatius, 'Pat Cahill' & two Auxiliaries. One of the Auxies just sat down and drank, the other man the notorious 'Splendid' kept singing drinking and falling. His oft repeated song was 'I love my love'. He felt delighted & honoured to be in the company of the Sinn Féiners who were fine soldiers and fine gentleman. 'If there had to be a fight again it would be a fight between gentlemen, 20 auxiliaries or 35 or 100 pitted against an equal number of Sinn Féiners. I let the decision rest with that victory.' 'What about the arms?' said Mr Carmody. 'An equal number of rifles or revolvers' said 'Splendid'. 'Then ye will be beaten' declared Mr Carmody.

To the question will Sinn Féin keep the Truce? Comdt O'Loughlin replied, 'Yes. The IRA Sinn Féiners are too honourable to break it, and those who would like to break it have not the courage to do it.'

At a meeting of the 5th Battalion Mid-Clare it was suggested that the Galwaymen serving with the 5th Unit would remain in Mid-Clare & I was informed that I would be in charge of a camp at Kilnamona. The Mid-Clare Brigade were proud of their achievements. They began the fight with 2 revolvers. The end came with the Flying Column alone in possession of 66 rifles and perhaps as many revolvers. They had victories to their credit at Ennis, Rinneen, Ruane, Monreal & Ballyvaughan. Their losses included Máirtín Devitt & Breen (killed in action) Lehane & Connole. The wounded included Ignatius ONeill, Peadar & Paddy O'Loughlin, Seán MacNamara, Dick Carroll (Constable) & Michael Killoughry. The enemy losses must have been much greater. The IRA houses burnt down were off set by the burning of RIC Barracks & loyalist houses towards the end of the struggle. The IRA did this reluctantly but the order came from Headquarters.[73] Receiving information that some military were travelling by train, a small number of picked men of 5th held up the train, but the soldiers did not travel. The IRA found some equipment and copies of the *Hue and Cry* & it so happened that myself was one of the 'wanted men'.

Whilst in this area we got orders to burn down two loyalist houses unoccupied at the time. The local shopkeeper was unfriendly (a Mr T— Y.) and I was sent to demand five gallons of Parafin oil. I knocked at the door and told the man I wanted five gls [gallons] of oil. He immediately took the keys and filled the required amount. A young boy had been waiting for me & we took the parafin to our comrades who had a quantity of Petrol. When night came we went on the work of destruction. The owner of the 1st house was a veterinary surgeon & hundreds of books several dealing with diseases and cures for horses were stored there. Pádraig Kilkelly was in charge & insisted on saturating the staircase with Petrol, which was regarded as very dangerous. However he took the necessary precautions. The petrol took fire & lit up until exhausted but the woodwork did not burn. After several trials the same result was obtained. The Parafin oil was also a failure. It was only when a quantity of hay was placed on the stairs that the woodwork took fire & then the house with books etc. A bearth of hay was taken to the other house and this kindled the fire. It was now almost dawn and a messenger arrived saying the crown forces were mobilized and that we were to leave immediately.

I applied for leave to come home a few times, but was refused. Pádraig Kilkelly said himself and Joe were going home and therefore I could not go. Paddy O'Loughlin was left in charge of the 5th Unit, but since the Truce things were left in obeyance [*sic*]. Seizing my opportunity I applied to Paddy O'Loughlin for leave to go home. 'I will give you leave' he said 'or any thing I can do for you. I'll be only too glad to do it.' I said goodbye to Mr & Mrs McCormick & children who had treated me with the greatest kindness. I took my Colt repeating rifle, for footwear I had a pair of Pampootees (úr-leathar) I had bought from an Aran man at Doolin and set out for Galway. I crossed Leamaneh, but began to tire as I found that pampootees were not suitable for walking across country. I came out on a boreen and saw a house nearby. After a while I entered & asked for a drink of water & the direction of way to Killanall. I kept crossing the fields until I reached a house where Pádraig Kilkelly had left my bicycle. I then cycled to the vicinity of Carrowkilleen. Night was falling and I hastened to the camp among the hazels where I stayed for the night. As my home had been burned down I got my meals at my sisters at Carrowkilleen but stayed alone at our tents at night which served as a quiet peaceable home among the hazels, hollies wild birds, rabbits and wild goats.

Re-organization

I did not go back to Clare, neither did the Kilkellys, Hynes & the others. A new organization scheme was launched. Michael Brennan was appointed Comdt of the 1st Western Division, Dave Reynolds Vice Cdt,[74] Seumas Hogan Div. IO. Joe Stankard was appointed Brg Comdt (South Galway),[75] Jack Fahy Vice Comdt, Dan Ryan Quarter Master, Pádraig Kilkelly in charge of Garda & I was appointed Brigade IO, which entitled me to attend Divisional Meetings. Money was collected and Training Camps established. Michael Collins was chief IO.[76]

I re-appointed my old IOs including Constable Durkin, Joe Togher, Tommy Fahy (Craughwell), Kil— Thos [*sic*] Stephenson (Connell), George Fahy (Athenry) & others, including the Manageress of a Galway hotel. I stayed at my cousin's house (Pat Keane) Gort, and occupied a room upstairs where I could check & rewrite and abridge the contents which I sent by rail (chiefly) to Div IO. I was congratulated by Mick Collins on my work whilst the Div IO complimented me every week on my reports. When in Galway I stayed at Toghers.

The messages required to be sent by rail I forwarded to Berty Powel, Athenry, who was in charge of this dept.

Gort Brigade

Since Liam Mellows placed his camp at Ballycahalan Sinn Féin was gathering strength despite the GAA split, & the members played their part in every phase of Sinn Féin activities.[77] Their losses included 2 men and a lady murdered by Crown Forces The houses burned down included, the Rural Hall (presented by Edward Martyn)[78] & 4 houses (2 partially), in Ardrahan Parish or Coy area, 4 in Kinvara, 4 in Ballycahalan (Kilbeacanty), and 2 in Peterswell (one partially).

The enemy losses included the Black & Tan chief, 2 military officers, 2 RIC men, a lady (all killed in ambushes), a spy, and an ex-RIC sergeant (father of an auxiliary officer) who was killed in a hand to hand fight with the local Sinn Féin Captain whilst all the RIC barracks in the area had been burned down.

Galway City

The inhabitants of Galway city held divergent political views. The leaders of the Sinn Féin side included George Nichols, Louis E. O'Dea, Micky Allen, Tom Hynes, Tom Flanagan, Seumas Carter & Michael McDonagh,[79] and their followers included those men & women who came from Castlegar, Claregalway, Moycullen & Connemara and worked & settled in Galway City

The loyalist leaders included W.F. & J.Y. & the sons of RIC who held remunerative & lucrative jobs.[80] As Salthill was described by a judge as the mecca of retired RIC & military, these with the redoubtable separation allowance women formed a numerous and aggressive section of the Community. W.J. was son of a recruiting sergeant and was an active & persuasive British agent. He tried to establish a 'Farmers' Battalion' for the enforcement of conscription which did not materialse. He sponsored the 'white Feather' resolution of the Galway Co. Council, although there was not a quorum present, just as the British Government was about to negotiate a Truce, and wrote the 'No Truck with Sinn Féin' article whilst posing as a follower of John Redmond.[81] It is generally acknowleged that the Galway resolution brought the Black & Tans to Ireland, and the most fiendish of these were sent to Galway. The RIC DIs Cruise & McGloinn were up to the Black & Tans standard in the organizing of murder & murder gangs. The victims included Fr Griffin, Seán Quirke, Mr Ml Walsh, Mr Moran Mr Folan and Mr Geoghegan. In a fight at the railway station Sinn Féin Volunteer McVeigh and the Black and Tan Krumm were both killed.

With the advent of the Truce Pádraig Kilkelly and myself were sent to Galway city to re-organize the local company. As we walked down Eglington Street we saw the Black & Tan 'Dindy' the centre of an admiring group of more than a dozen women and girls. Seeing us approaching in uniforms 'Dindy' said aloud with astonishment 'Sinn Féiners, Sinn Féiners. — Evidently Sinn Féiners.'

It was no trouble to organize the Galway company whilst the other companies of the Battallion which included Castlegar Claregalway and Oranmore were throroughly organized already. The first evening the officers of the Galway Co[mpany] were appointed, Cunningham was appointed captain. The Coy turned out for drill every evening & went through the usual coy drill.

I concentrated on IO work. I visited the manageress every night to find out what Tans were there that day, what they were saying, etc. One night Joe Togher said he got word that we were to be shot on our way to Salthill, but Fr Tom Burke said 'I'll go with ye and ye will not be shot.' On reaching the hotel Fr Burke returned to town. I entered the hotel whilst Joe did sentry as usual & nothing happened.

IOs

It is generally recognized that the most bitter & most potent enemies of Irish National movements were the RIC. They were heartless in aiding the evictions and bludgeoned the Irish people. But physical force was not their most potent weapon — And whilst the people generally kept them at arms length, they married Irish women & courted Irish girls, and by lying and sycophancy they got a good amount of information which they forwarded to the British Government.

In the early days of Sinn Féin, Cahal Brew [*sic*][82] had handbills boycotting the RIC distributed throughout the country, and with the advent of the Sinn Féin Volunteers this boycott was intensified. Then it was decided to meet the methods of the RIC at their own game; the man in charge of this work was Mick Collins. Soon he had the best secret service men England had, working for him including Broy, Nevill [*recte* Neligan], Macnamara and others.[83] He also appointed IO & SS officers throughout the country. I succeeded in organizing these service[s] in my brigade.

RIC in general Constable Durkin

Local Con[stable]s McDermott, Ardrahan; Molloy (Cruise's Bodyguard)

Auxiliaries — Manageress of K hotel, Galway

Castle Agents — J.Y. OBE — Mr Kilbride
W.F. — S. Carter

P.O. Letters Joe Togher, Galway

Galway City Mr I.

Craughwell — Tommy Fahy

Gort — H. Shaughnessy, M. Connell

Telegrams — Joe Quinn

Athenry — George Fahy

Rail Service — Berty Powel, Athenry; Mr Hough, Limerick

Ardrahan — P. Shaughnessy

Auxiliary Reports — Constable Kearney

The RIC Head-Constables had charge of the Secret Service and Constable Durcan deciphered the codes and wrote the reports for the Head Constables. He noted down the length of service of certain RIC men, what they did, their height age & colour of eyes & hair. These he sent me & photos. Joe Togher copied names & addresses of the Auxiliaries as well as their home addresses, & made out an alphabetical list. Manageress Photos of Auxiliaries with names, their deeds sayings & writings.

Kill B[ride] was bosom friend of J.Y. & noted down everything said by him.

Tommy Fahy — made use of a tailor named Teirney who drank with Tans & Peelers.

Constable Kearney typed reports of secret service work done by Auxiliaries.

The Auxiliaries' reports were largely imagination. One report asserted that the Sinn Féin clubs in South Galway were reduced to 4, the strongest being the new Branch at Béal Aba, and that their IO was T. Fahy. The name Fahy is about the commonest name in South Galway, and the Christian names of Mary, Brighid, Paddy, Mike, Jack and Tommy Fahy are as plentiful as blackberries. Note — Béal Abha (meaning mouth of river) is beside the Cloon waterfall a short distance from the house of Tommy Doonarty (angl. 'Davenport') Some neighbours used come there (cuairt — visiting). Cloon is in Kilbeacanty Parish & the villagers of Cloon & Streamstown belonged to Kilbeacanty club.

The advent of ex-soldiers into the Sinn Féin movement took the Volunteers away somewhat from the Sinn Féin ideals. These men were fine experienced soldiers, were whiskey drinkers, cursed and swore and were rough and reckless, and also had a winning way about them and were able to get the less experienced Sinn Féiners to look up to them for advice. During the truce an auxiliary officer was in virtual control of Rennmore Barracks, an ex-Black Watch soldier was in virtual charge of Gort Barracks. A Black & Tan was companion of one of the best known and bravest Sinn Féin soldier[s] in County Galway. In like manner, prominent Sinn Féin men & women were to be seen in the company of Peelers' sons & daughters. If a Black & Tan or a Peeler gave information or arms to the Volunteers he was entitled to payment in cash, but he was not entitled to be placed over the local IRA man. Fr Moran was shocked when he saw a body of IRA men in Crossley Tenders. These he declared should have been burned as the demon spirit remained in them & the IRA men looked like Tans. A man he said was drilling an IRA company in Eyre Square. All these men knew Irish but the language used was the language of the Cockney Tommy 'Slow-hip awms', and so also we kept the pennies with the head of the famine queen in our pockets, kept Dublin Castle & the permanent officials of the Crown to run the country. No wonder the British Government succeeded in getting the invincible Sinn Féin soldiers to turn the guns on each other and kindle the fires of envy and hatred widespread. The auxiliary officer Br— who shot Fr Griffin spoke the truth when he said to Miss W[alshe] that there would be a slaughter of Sinn Féiners soon & when she said 'That cannot be as ye are going' [he replied:] 'It is no joke, the Sinn Féiners will slaughter each other. It is all arranged and you will find that what I say is true.'

I was proceeding to Toormakeady Connacht College to take up duty as Ollamh, (Tommy Collins was to come with me as student) when we met Peadar O'Loughlin (Comdt). He had a dispatch to the effect that I was to re-organize the IRB in Co. Galway with the exception of Connemara where Colm Ó Gaora was appointed for similar work. I had no trouble in re-organizing the IRB and we held a meeting in Tuam of the Connacht IRB men. Seán Ó Murthuile[84] all Ireland organizer was present. Mícheál Ó Droighneamh, Colm Ó Gaora. T. Mac an Airchine,[85] S. Ó Ruadhain & myself represented Galway, Tom Ruane & Mr Walsh and a number of others represented the other counties. Mícheál Ó Droighneamh was appointed Chief Centre. It was suggested to me that the IRB should approve of the treaty; I replied that the IRB should be the last organization to approve and not the first.

I was about to set out for Limerick when I got a wire from Liam Mellows to meet him in Athenry the following day. I did go to Limerick, did my business and took 1st train for Galway at daybreak next morning. Tommy Fahy met me at Craughwell and informed me that I was to get off and go to Killeeneen. Liam Mellows, Eamon Corbett, Hare Callanan & Mattie Neilan were at Walshe's. They seemed moody irritable and undecided. When I said that it was time to be starting for meeting in Loughrea I got no answer. They seemed careless and despondent. At long last we started for Loughrea and arrived late. The Comhairle Ceanntair had approved of the treaty.

At a later meeting called to appoint delegates to all-Ireland Convention I was proceeding to Loughrea on bicycle when I was overtaken at Kilchreest by John Nolan & the Kilmacduagh delegates. They were all for the treaty although I held a meeting in Tirneevin a few nights previously and urged them to vote against it. They took me in the car and were just in time for the meeting. It was proposed that the delegate appointed be instructed to vote for treaty. I proposed as an amendment that the delegate to Dublin Convention be instructed to vote against acceptance of Treaty. Certain knotty questions were then asked whereupon Tommy Reidy of Kinvara produced a slip or cutting from paper in answer to the questions. We won by one vote.

Then Tommy Reidy proposed that I be the delegate and this was agreed to.

An agreement was reached at the Dublin Convention and the coming election was dubbed the Pact Election.[86]

The election was coming on when Frank Barrett informed me that I was appointed Divisional IO and should take up duty at Ennis. I was getting ready for Ennis when Miss Caisil[87] called saying she wanted me as Election Agent for South Galway, that she had Colm O'Geary for Connemara & Jack O'Neill for North Galway. I told her I was taking up duty at Ennis. She said she would get permission. I went with her to Crusheen to Seán Macnamara and the three of us went to Ennis to Frank Barrett. The Comdt said I could appoint substitute in Ennis for the time being and that I could carry on both jobs as Galway was in the Division. It was thought that the same TDs would be returned as at last Election, but the Teachers put forward a Mr O'Connell to represent Labour. John Coen was appointed Election Agent for South Galway for Free State Side. George Nichols, Hare Callinan and their supporters were very active as also were O'Connell and his supporters — But I got a shock when I met Liam Mellowes and Frank Fahy. Both refused to hold any meetings, to canvass or do anything to further their interests as candidates. I told them that the electors would become careless if they did not meet them, and would consider they were being made little of. I got a bigger shock when I heard former Sinn Féin officers boosting O'Connell. It was a fight between Liam Mellowes and Frank Fahy for the last seat. Had they gone round to the people they would head the poll. Frank Fahy was elected.

I received a letter of congratulations from Head Quarters and a flattering letter from Miss Caisil saying she made use of my reports to show how scheme of work should be laid & reports written.

Abbreviations

CI	County Inspector, RIC
CO	Colonial Office
DI	District Inspector RIC
DMP	Dublin Metropolitan Police
HO	Home Office
MCR	Monthly Confidential Reports, RIC County Inspectors
NAI	National Archives, Dublin
NLI	National Library of Ireland, Dublin
PRO	Public Record Office, London
RIC	Royal Irish Constabulary
UIL	United Irish League

Notes to Introduction

1 Michael Laffan, *The Partition of Ireland, 1911–1925* (Dundalk, 1987), ch. 2; Michael Tierney, *Eoin MacNeill: Scholar and Man of Action, 1867–1945*, ed. F. X. Martin (Oxford, 1980), pp. 97–124; Seán Ó Lúing, *I Die in a Good Cause: A Study of Thomas Ashe, Idealist and Revolutionary* (Tralee, 1970), pp. 67–72.

2 Laurence M. Geary, *The Plan of Campaign, 1856–1891* (Cork, 1986), app. 5, p. 185; Paul Bew, *Conflict and Conciliation in Ireland, 1890–1910: Parnellites and Radical Agrarians* (Oxford, 1987), pp. 146–7.

3 NAI, Census 1901, Co. of Galway, 90/13, Form B. 2: 'Return of Out-Offices and Farm-Steadings'; Marie McNamara and Maura Madden (eds), *Beagh: A History and a Heritage* (Beagh, 1995), ch. 9.

4 Pádraig Ó Fathaigh married Maighréad Ní Chonaing on 12 September 1922.

5 Timothy G. McMahon, 'The Gaelic League and the Irish-Ireland Movement' (M.A. thesis, University of Wisconsin–Madison, 1994), pp. 107–13; NAI, Census 1911, Co. of Galway, 90/13, Form A.

6 Ó Fathaigh Memoir, pp. 1, 88–9: NLI, Ó Fathaigh Papers, MS 21288; Ó Fathaigh Irish-Language Memoir, pp. 1–5: ibid. See also Donncha Ó Súilleabháin, *Na Timirí i ré Tosaigh an Chonartha, 1893–1927* (Dublin, 1990); Colm Ó Cearúil, *Aspail ar son na Gaeilge: Timirí Chonradh na Gaeilge, 1899–1923* (Dublin, 1995).

7 Ó Cearúil, *Aspail*, pp. 139–40; Colm Ó Gaora, *Mise* (Dublin, 1943), p. 115.

8 C. Desmond Greaves, *Liam Mellows and the Irish Revolution* (London, 1971), pp. 72–4; Bew, *Conflict and Conciliation*, p. 147; Tierney, *MacNeill*, pp. 124–55. See

also RIC Crime Branch Special, Précis, Nov. 1913: PRO, CO 904/119; CI, Galway West Riding, Monthly Confidential Report [henceforth MCR], Oct. 1914: ibid., CO 904/120.

9 See W. J. Lowe and E. L. Malcolm, 'The Domestication of the Royal Irish Constabulary, 1836–1922', *Irish Economic and Social History*, xix (1992), pp. 27–48; Kent Fedorowich, 'The Problem of Disbandment: The Royal Irish Constabulary and Imperial Migration, 1919–29', *Irish Historical Studies*, xxx (1996–97), pp. 88–110.

10 J. Anthony Gaughan, *Austin Stack: Portrait of a Separatist* (Dublin, 1977), p. 43; Greaves, *Mellows*, p. 75.

11 Greaves, *Mellows*, pp. 88–9; Pádraic O'Farrell, *Who's Who in the Irish War of Independence and Civil War, 1916–1923* (Dublin, 1997), p. 79.

12 Greaves, *Mellows*, pp. 89–94; Desmond Ryan, *The Rising: The Complete Story of Easter Week* (3rd ed., Dublin, 1957), pp. 244–8, 265–7. See also Reports filed by CIs at the Request of the RIC Inspector General on the State of the Counties during 1916: PRO, CO 904/120.

13 Florence O'Donoghue (ed.), *Sworn To Be Free: The Complete Book of IRA Jailbreaks, 1918–1921* (Tralee, 1971), p. 9; Seán O'Mahony, *Frongoch: University of Revolution* (Dublin, 1987), pp. 19–26.

14 Charles Townshend, *The British Campaign in Ireland, 1919–1921* (Oxford, 1975), p. 1. See also MCR, Mar. 1918: PRO, CO 904/105.

15 Townshend, *British Campaign*, pp. 1–27; O'Donoghue (ed.), *Sworn To Be Free*, pp. 19–25; MCRs, Apr.–May 1918: PRO, CO 904/105–6.

16 MCR, Dec. 1918: PRO CO 904/107.

17 MCR, Oct. 1917: ibid., CO 904/104; MCR, July 1918: ibid., CO 904/106; MCR, Sept. 1919: ibid., CO 904/110.

18 MCR, Aug. 1918: ibid., CO 904/106; MCR, Oct. 1918: ibid., CO 904/107; MCR, June 1919: ibid., CO 904/109; Dan Breen, *My Fight for Irish Freedom* (Dublin, 1924), pp. 34–49; *The Times*, 18 Dec. 1920.

19 Joost Augusteijn, *From Public Defiance to Guerilla Warfare: The Experience of Ordinary Volunteers in the Irish War of Independence, 1916–1921* (London, 1996), pp. 353–67; Peter Hart, *The IRA and Its Enemies: Violence and Community in Cork, 1916–1923* (Oxford, 1998), pp. 154–73; David Fitzpatrick, *Politics and Irish Life, 1913–1921: Provincial Experience of War and Revolution* (Dublin, 1977), pp. 17, 20–28, 168–70, 200–21; Michael Brennan, *The War in Clare, 1911–1921: Personal Memoirs of the Irish War of Independence* (Exeter, 1980), pp. 25–7, 36–44, 70–71; Richard Bennett, *The Black and Tans* (New York, 1959), pp. 37–9; Ernie O'Malley, *Army Without Banners / On Another Man's Wound* (London, 1965 ed.), pp. 105–7; Townshend, *British Campaign*, pp. 14–20, 40–46; McNamara and Madden (eds), *Beagh*, pp. 114–17.

20 Brennan, *War in Clare*, pp. 15–17.

21 See Ó Gaora, *Mise*, p. 160; Tierney, *MacNeill*, p. 241.

22 Earl of Longford and T. P. O'Neill, *Eamon de Valera* (London, 1970), pp. 52–9; Gaughan, *Stack*, pp. 69–71; Tierney, *MacNeill*, pp. 242–52; Ó Lúing, *I Die in a Good Cause*, pp. 95–114.

23 MCR, Nov. 1917: PRO, CO 904/104; copy of the bill of fare for the dinner at Nevin's Hotel, Loughrea, 1 Nov. 1917, provided to the editor by the Ó Fathaigh family.

24 MCR, Feb. 1918: PRO, CO 904/105.

25 MCR, June 1919: ibid., CO 904/109. See also *Irish Independent*, 27 June, 1, 3, 4, 7 July 1919.

26 MCRs, July–Dec. 1919: PRO, CO 904/109–10.

27 Townshend, *British Campaign*, pp. 49–50. See also MCR, Feb. 1920: PRO, CO 904/111.

28 Dorothy Macardle, *The Irish Republic* (New York, 1965 ed.), pp. 344–5; Bennett, *Black and Tans*, pp. 40–42; Arthur Mitchell, *Revolutionary Government in Ireland: Dail Éireann, 1919–22* (Dublin, 1995), pp. 129–30; Townshend, *British Campaign*, p. 76.

29 Ó Fathaigh Irish-Language Memoir, p. 11: NLI, Ó Fathaigh Papers, MS 21288; *The Times*, 26 Apr. 1920; *Irish Independent*, 10 May 1920; *Hansard* 5, cxxviii, 834 (26 Apr. 1920).

30 *Hansard* 5, cxxviii, 1337–78 (28 Apr. 1920). See also *The Times*, 30 Apr., 5 May 1920; *Irish Independent*, 28 Apr., 1, 3, 5 May 1920.

31 *Hansard* 5, cxxviii, 1344–5 (28 Apr. 1920).

32 *Irish Independent*, 5, 20 May 1920.

33 *Hansard* 5, cxxviii, 1367 (28 Apr. 1920); A.W. Brian Simpson, *In the Highest Degree Odious: Detention without Trial in Wartime Britain* (Oxford, 1992), pp. 15–33.

34 Bennett, *Black and Tans*, p. 44; Macardle, *Irish Republic*, p. 345; Mitchell, *Revolutionary Government*, p. 130; *Irish Independent*, 21, 22, 27 May 1920.

35 *Irish Independent*, 18, 19 May 1920; *Hansard* 5, cxxx, 576–7 (10 June 1920).

36 O'Donoghue (ed.), *Sworn To Be Free*, p. 8; *Hansard* 5, cxxx, 2176 (23 June 1920); *The Times*, 20 Aug. 1920. The announcement of 23 June applied to convicted prisoners, but the government later extended the policy to incorporate interned prisoners as well. See *The Times*, 20 Aug. 1920.

37 O'Donoghue (ed.), *Sworn To Be Free*, 10–11.

38 All three cases are discussed in typewritten notes which may have been intended for inclusion in the memoir. The notes are in possession of Ó Fathaigh's family, who graciously shared a copy with the editor. See also O'Farrell, *Who's Who*, p. 48; *The Times*, 22 Oct., 30 Nov., 6 Dec. 1920.

39 Fitzpatrick, *Politics and Irish Life*, p. 225.

40 'Report of the British Labour Commission to Ireland', *The Nation*, cxii, no. 2899 (26 Jan.1921), p. 134.

41 *Lady Gregory's Journals*, ed. Daniel J. Murphy (London, 1978), pp. 187–215; *Irish Independent*, 24, 27, 28, 29 Sept. 1920; *The Times*, 21, 22 Oct. 1920.

42 *Lady Gregory's Journals*, pp. 197–202; *Irish Independent*, 5, 6, 9, 18 Nov. 1920; *The Times*, 5 Nov. 1920.

43 O'Farrell, *Who's Who*, pp.39–40; *Irish Independent*, 17–20, 22–24 Nov. 1920; F. P. Crozier, *Ireland for Ever* (London, 1932), pp. 107–8.

44 *Lady Gregory's Journals*, pp. 206, 213; *Irish Independent*, 24 Sept., 26 Nov. 1920.

45 Townshend, *British Campaign*, p. 111; *Lady Gregory's Journals*, pp. 217, 255–74; *The Times*, 17 May 1921; *Irish Independent*, 17, 18, 19 May 1921; Sir Ormonde Winter, *Winter's Tale: An Autobiography* (London, 1955), pp. 312–15; RIC Report on the Ballyturin Tragedy: PRO, CO 904/121; Proceedings of the Court of Enquiry and Certificates of Finding: ibid., HO 351/77.

46 *Irish Independent*, 17, 18, 19 May 1921.

47 *Connacht Tribune*, 2 Dec. 1933, 10 Feb., 3 Mar. 1934, 3 Apr., 31 Aug. 1937, 26 Mar. 1976. See also Ó Fathaigh Irish-Language Memoir, pp. 14–19: NLI, Ó Fathaigh Papers, MS 21288.

Notes to Narrative

1 Liam Mellows (1892–1922). IRB and Volunteer organiser; Commandant, County Galway Volunteers during Easter Rising, 1916; IRA Director of Purchases during War of Independence; TD for County Galway, 1918–22; opposed Treaty.

2 George Nicholls (Galway city). Solicitor; IRB member; member of Sinn Féin Executive, 1910; pro-Treaty TD for County Galway, 1922. Laurence Lardner (Athenry, Co. Galway). Publican; IRB centre; member of IRB Supreme Council for Connacht, 1917. Michael Joseph Howley (1895–1920). Volunteer and IRB member; court martialled, 1916; killed, Dublin, 4 Dec. 1920.

3 Meeting of January 1916 at which Pearse informed Volunteer and IRB leaders from Counties Galway, Clare and Limerick of plans for the Easter Rising.

4 Eoin MacNeill (1867–1945). Scholar and patriot; founded Gaelic League, 1893, and Irish Volunteers, 1913.

5 Rev. Henry Feeney, Clarinbridge, Co. Galway. Chaplain of County Galway Volunteers; handled dispatches during Easter Rising, 1916.

6 Rev. J. W. O'Meehan, CC, Kinvara, 1916. Volunteer officer; Sinn Féin enthusiast.

7 H. H. Asquith (1852–1928). British Liberal politician and statesman; Prime Minister, 1908–16; visited Ireland, 12–18 May 1916.

8 John Coen (Gort, Co. Galway). Interned at Frongoch, 1916.

9 Colm Ó Gaora (1887–1954). Republican; language enthusiast, educator and author; opposed Treaty.

10 Francis Fahy (1879–1953). Politician, educator, language enthusiast; Ceann Comhairle of Dáil Éireann, 1932.

11 Traditional exchange of greetings in Irish.

12 Michael Fleming (Clarinbridge, Co. Galway). Described by Greaves as 'the old Fenian Michael Fleming' (Greaves, *Mellows*, p. 74, 89). Participant in Easter Rising in County Galway, 1916.

13 James Connolly (1868–1916). Socialist organiser and journalist; leader of the Irish Citizen Army; executed 12 May 1916.

14 Short-lived breakaway faction of IRB responsible for Phoenix Park murders, 6 May 1882.

15 Seán Heuston (1891–1916). Volunteer Commandant at Mendicity Institute, Usher's Island, 1916; executed 8 May 1916.

16 Seán Mac Diarmada (1884–1916). Treasurer, Supreme Council, IRB; signatory of the 1916 Proclamation; executed 12 May 1916.

17 Eamon de Valera (1882–1975). Revolutionary; politician; President of the Dáil, 1919–21, and of the Irish Republic, 1921–22.

18 Many of these prisoners played prominent roles in the founding of the Irish state. Among them were Robert Brennan (1881–1964), politician and diplomat; Austin Stack (1879–1929), revolutionary republican noted for multiple hunger-strikes; Desmond FitzGerald (1888–1947), writer, revolutionary and statesman; Thomas Ashe (1885–1917), teacher, republican and language enthusiast; Seán MacEntee (1889–1984), politician and poet, who served as Tánaiste 1959–65; Diarmuid Lynch (1878–1950), republican, author and language enthusiast. For further information on these and others listed see O'Farrell, *Who's Who.*

19 Among the Portland prisoners listed are William Cosgrave (1880–1965), revolutionary politician and President of the Executive Council of the Irish Free State 1922–32; Piaras Béaslaí (1881–1965), language enthusiast, revolutionary and writer.

20 Geoffrey Keating (*c.* 1570 – *c.* 1650). Poet and historian, whose best-known work is *Foras Feasa ar Éireann*.

21 J. J. Walsh. GAA enthusiast and member of the Hibernian Rifles; Postmaster General and Minister for Posts and Telegraphs in the 1920s.

22 This journal was entitled *An Buabhall* [*The Bugle*].

23 Sir Roger Casement (1864–1916). Officer of the British colonial service and Irish patriot; envoy of Clan na Gael to Germany; executed 3 August 1916.

24 Arthur Lynch (1861–1934). Australian-Irish IRB member, journalist and author; elected MP for Galway City, 1901; sentenced to death on a charge of treason, 1902, later commuted to one year's imprisonment.

25 Now Pearse Station.

26 Major William Redmond (1861–1917). Nationalist politician, brother of John Redmond; MP for East Clare; killed in action with British army on Western Front during First World War.

27 Polling day was 11 July 1917. De Valera defeated Lynch by 5,010 votes to 2,035 votes.

28 Michael Brennan (1896–1986). Soldier and author; commanded East Clare Brigade of the IRA during War of Independence; named Commandant of 1st Western Division, IRA, 1921; subsequently Chief of Staff of the National Army.

29 Pádhraig Ó Domhnalláin (1884–1960). Irish-language enthusiast, educator and journalist; headmaster, Toormakeady Irish College, 1908–20.

30 In April 1919 the First Dáil set out to raise £250,000 to fund government and army activities through a public sale of bonds. Co-ordinated by the Minister for Finance, Michael Collins, the campaign raised more than £370,000.

31 Seán Mac Énrí's *Gearr-Scríobhadh na Gaedhilge*, modelled after the standard English shorthand guide, Sir Isaac Pitman's *Shorthand Instructor*.

32 The initial letter in the sequence was written by Fr Brennan, then CC of the parish of Ahascragh and Caltra, and appeared in the *Irish Independent* on 27 June 1919.

33 District Inspector Vincent W. T. Scully, stationed at Portumna, Co. Galway.

34 Philip Waldron (1874–1952). Language enthusiast and educator.

35 Rev. J. Dignam, D.D., Administrator of the parish of Duniry and Kilnelaghan; lived at Abbey, Co. Galway.

36 Pádhraig Kilkelly (Towna, Kinvara, Co. Galway). Interned at Frongoch, 1916; Commandant of the Kinvara Company of the Irish Volunteers; Chairman of Gort Rural District Council; *ex-officio* member of Galway County Council.

37 William Hynes (Dungory, Kinvara, Co. Galway). Several Hyneses appear in Ó Fathaigh's story. William and Michael served with him in the IRA. Their father, Patsy, had hosted Ó Fathaigh's Irish classes in Kinvara. And Patsy's brother Tomás was himself a teacher of Irish. He is occasionally referred to in the text as Tomás Ó h-Eidhin.

38 Patrick Loughnane (1891?–1920). Captain of the Shanaglish Company of the Irish Volunteers and President of the local Sinn Féin branch; arrested and killed, Nov. 1920.

39 Séamus Murphy. Commandant, Galway Brigade, Irish Volunteers, 1917.

40 Francis Shawe-Taylor (1869–1920). Galway landowner and horseman; killed 3 Mar. 1920.

41 Martin Finnerty (Caltragh, Gurteen, Co. Galway). Former secretary of East Galway UIL; member of Galway County Council.

42 John Redmond (1856–1918). Nationalist politician and leader of the Irish Parliamentary Party, 1900–18.

43 Mícheál Breathnach (1881–1908). Language enthusiast and founder of Toormakeady Irish College.

44 Sir Antony MacDonnell (1844–1925). Under-Secretary for Ireland, 1902–8.

45 Edward Shortt (1862–1935). Chief Secretary for Ireland, 1918–19; Home Secretary, 1919–22.

46 St Marylebone Infirmary, London, colloquially known as Marleybone.

47 William O'Brien (1852–1928). Journalist, orator, land activist and parliamentarian; founded the 'All for Ireland League' in 1910.

48 David Lloyd George (1863–1945). Liberal politician and statesman; coalition Prime Minister, 1916–22. *Hansard* contains no record of Lloyd George having been questioned about the Wormwood Scrubs prisoners.

49 Joseph Dowling had been recruited by Sir Roger Casement to join in the Irish rebellion against Britain while a prisoner-of-war in Germany. On 12 April 1918 police arrested Dowling on Crab Island, where he had been left by a German submarine. This arrest served as the pretext for the government's sweeping arrests and deportations of dozens of Sinn Féin political leaders on 17–18 May 1918.

50 Peadar Clancy (?–1920). Shopkeeper and Vice-Commandant, Dublin Brigade, IRA; captured and killed on night of 20–21 Nov. 1920.

51 Proposed on 3 December 1920 by James Haverty (Springlawn, Moylough, Co. Galway), this statement called for a negotiated settlement of the Troubles; Lloyd George used it as a pretext to push ahead with armed confrontation, despite opening informal peace talks with the Vice-President of Sinn Féin, Father Michael O'Flanagan. Kilkelly's letter denouncing the resolution appeared in the *Irish Independent*, 13 Dec. 1920.

52 Mrs Eileen Quinn (Ardrahan, Co. Galway). Pregnant mother of three, killed on 1 Nov. 1920.

53 Tomás Malone (Tyrrellspass, Co. Westmeath). Interned at Frongoch, 1916; IRA Brigade Commandant in East Limerick area during War of Independence; opposed Treaty; served on IRA executive until 1938.

54 Rev. J. Nagle, PP, Beagh, Gort, Co. Galway.

55 Harry Loughnane (1897?–1920). Secretary of Sinn Féin branch at Shanaglish, Co. Galway.

56 Patsy Hynes's barn, Dungory, Kinvara.

57 Dr T. J. Connolly. Dispensary doctor stationed at Kinvara.

58 See *Irish Independent*, 7, 8, 9 Dec. 1920.

59 Constable McDermott, Ó Fathaigh's contact in Ardrahan, sent messages through Miss Hanbury, a neighbour of the Hynes family.

60 District Inspector C. E. N. Blake (?–1921). Captain, stationed at Gort, Co. Galway, in late autumn 1920.

61 Constable Patrick Durkan (1874–?). Born Co. Mayo; joined RIC in 1894; served in west Cork (1894–1908) and in west Galway (1908–22).

62 Peadar O'Loughlin. Commandant, 5th Battalion, Mid-Clare Brigade, IRA; later promoted to Brigade Adjutant under Commandant Frank Barrett.

63 Frank and Joe Barrett (Daragh, Co. Clare). Brothers in command of Mid-Clare Brigade during War of Independence; opposed Treaty, with Frank serving as a member of the anti-treaty IRA Executive.

64 Seán MacNamara (Ballyvaughan, Co. Clare). Commandant, 6th Battalion, Mid-Clare Brigade, IRA.

65 Danny Allman (?–1921). Commandant, Kerry No. 2 Brigade, IRA; killed during attack on British provisions train at Headfort Junction, 3 Mar. 1921.

66 The Ballyvaughan attack occurred on 21 May 1921.

67 Probably Very Rev. Patrick Canon Hannon, PP, Kilfarboy, Milltown Malbay, Co. Clare. The failed attack at Dysert took place on 17 May 1921.

68 Claude Albert Chavasse (1886–1971). Scholar, Irish-language enthusiast and political activist. The Athenry procession took place on 14 November 1915, attended by more than 1,000 people.

69 Spelled elsewhere as Kearney.

70 Mrs Margaret Gregory. Sole survivor of the Ballyturin ambush; daughter-in-law of playwright and folklorist Isabella Augusta, Lady Gregory (1852–1932) of Coole Park; widow of Lieutenant William Robert Gregory (1881–1918), whose death inspired W. B. Yeats's poem 'An Irish Airman Foresees his Death'; married Captain Guy Gough in September 1928.

71 The funeral was on 15 May 1921.

72 Ignatius O'Neill. Commandant, 4th Battalion, Mid-Clare Brigade, IRA.

73 On 22 June 1921 the IRA General Headquarters issued a general order authorising brigade commandants to burn the homes of 'the most active enemies of Ireland' as a counter to government reprisals against the homes and property of republicans.

74 Dave Reynolds. Pro-Treaty officer wounded while storming Limerick Castle, July 1922; General Officer Commanding Free State forces in Cork.

75 Joe Stanford (Ballybane, Gort, Co. Galway). Chairman, Gort Poor Law Board of Guardians; opposed Treaty.

76 Michael Collins (1890–1922). Revolutionary leader; Minister for Finance; Director of Intelligence, IRA; Chairman, Supreme Council, IRB; leading proponent of the Anglo-Irish Treaty; killed, Béal na mBláth, Co. Cork, 22 Aug. 1922.

77 In 1916 the Galway County Committee of the GAA split over a ruling involving the use of facilities in Loughrea. The factions reunited in 1921.

78 Edward Martyn (1859–1923). Playwright and Irish-language enthusiast; President of the National Council and then Sinn Féin, 1904–8; presented a parish hall to the people of Ardrahan for Gaelic League and community social functions.

79 Among those identified, Louis E. O'Dea served on Galway Urban District Council, while Michael McDonagh of Headford served on Galway County Council.

80 W.F. was possibly William Flaherty, who served on Galway Urban District Council for the South Ward; while, J.Y. was Joseph S. Young, OBE, who served on the Urban District Council for the city's North Ward.

81 Ó Fathaigh appears to be refering to James Haverty, the sponsor of the 'white feather' resolution, though his use of the abbreviation 'W.J.' obscures this.

82 Cathal Brugha (1874–1922). Revolutionary and Irish-language enthusiast; Chief of Staff of the IRA and Minister for Defence, 1919–22; opposed Treaty.

83 Colonel Eamonn Broy (1887–1972), detective, G Division, DMP; later Commissioner of the Garda Síochána. David Neligan, detective, G Division, DMP; attached to British Secret Service, 1921. James Macnamara, detective, Dublin Castle.

84 Seán Ó Murthuile (1881–1941). Republican and Gaelic League organiser; Secretary, Supreme Council, IRB; supported Treaty.

85 Thomas McInerney (Cahermore, Co. Galway). Commandant, South Galway Brigade, IRA; later Commandant, 2nd Battalion, South Galway Brigade.

86 The Sinn Féin Ard-Fheis opened on 21 February 1922 and focused on the Articles of Agreement with Britain. Initially a majority seemed opposed. Between the first and second days of the convention the executive met in closed session and negotiated a three-month delay to prepare a constitution for the new Irish state, preserving the appearance of a united Sinn Féin party. A similar obfuscation was the basis for the electoral pact agreed to by Michael Collins and Eamon de Valera in anticipation of the 1922 general election. In the event, Collins refused to honour the pact and only published the constitution on the eve of the election.

87 Possibly Alice Cashell (Cashel, Connemara). *Ex-officio* member of Galway County Council.

Bibliography

Augusteijn, Joost, *From Public Defiance to Guerrilla Warfare: The Experience of Ordinary Volunteers in the Irish War of Independence, 1916–1921* (London, 1996)

Bew, Paul, *Conflict and Conciliation in Ireland, 1890–1910: Parnellites and Radical Agrarians* (Oxford, 1987)

Barry, Tom, *Guerrilla Days in Ireland* (Dublin, 1949)

Bennett, Richard, *The Black and Tans* (New York, 1959)

Boyce, D. G., *Englishmen and Irish Troubles: British Public Opinion and the Making of Irish Policy, 1918–1922* (London, 1972)

Breen, Dan, *My Fight for Irish Freedom* (Dublin, 1924)

Brennan, Michael, *The War in Clare, 1911–1921: Personal Memoirs of the Irish War of Independence* (Exeter, 1980)

Crozier, F. P., *Ireland for Ever* (London, 1932)

Fitzpatrick, David, *Politics and Irish Life, 1913–1921: Provincial Experience of War and Revolution* (Dublin, 1977; 2nd ed., Cork, 1998)

Gaughan, J. Anthony, *Austin Stack: Portrait of a Separatist* (Dublin, 1977)

Greaves, C. Desmond, *Liam Mellows and the Irish Revolution* (London, 1971)

Gregory, Augusta, Lady, *Lady Gregory's Journals*, vol. i: *10 October 1916 – 24 February 1925*, ed. Daniel J. Murphy (London, 1978)

Hart, Peter, *The IRA and Its Enemies: Violence and Community in Cork, 1916–1923* (Oxford, 1998)

Laffan, Michael, *The Partition of Ireland, 1911–1925* (Dundalk, 1987)

Macardle, Dorothy, *The Irish Republic: A Documented Chronicle of the Anglo-Irish Conflict and the Partitioning of Ireland, with a Detailed Account of the Period 1916–1923* (New York, 1965 ed.)

McMahon, Timothy G., 'The Gaelic League and the Irish-Ireland Movement' M.A. thesis, University of Wisconsin–Madison, 1994)

McNamara, Marie, and Madden, Maura (eds), *Beagh: A History and a Heritage* (Beagh, 1995)

Mitchell, Arthur, *Revolutionary Government in Ireland: Dáil Éireann, 1919–22* (Dublin, 1995)

Ó Cearúil, Colm, *Aspail ar son na Gaeilge: Timirí Chonradh na Gaeilge, 1899–1923* (Dublin, 1995)

O'Donoghue, Florence, *No Other Law: The Story of Liam Lynch and the Irish Republican Army, 1916–1923* (Dublin, 1954)

—— (ed.), *Sworn To Be Free: The Complete Book of IRA Jailbreaks, 1918–1921* (Tralee, 1971)

O'Farrell, Pádraic, *Who's Who in the Irish War of Independence and Civil War, 1916–1923* (Dublin, 1997)

Ó Gaora, Colm, *Mise* (Dublin, 1943)

Ó Lúing, Seán, *I Die in a Good Cause: A Study of Thomas Ashe, Idealist and Revolutionary* (Tralee, 1970)

O'Mahony, Seán, *Frongoch: University of Revolution* (Dublin, 1987)

O'Malley, Ernie, *Army Without Banners / On Another Man's Wound* (London, 1965 ed.)

Ó Súilleabháin, Donncha, *Na Timirí i ré Tosaigh an Chonartha, 1893–1927* (Dublin, 1990)

Simpson, A. W. Brian, *In the Highest Degree Odious: Detention without Trial in Wartime Britain* (Oxford, 1992)

Tierney, Michael, *Eoin MacNeill: Scholar and Man of Action, 1867–1945*, ed. F. X. Martin (Oxford, 1980)

Townshend, Charles, *The British Campaign in Ireland, 1919–1921: The Development of Political and Military Policies* (Oxford, 1975)

Williams, T. Desmond (ed.), *The Irish Struggle, 1916–1926* (London, 1966)

Winter, Sir Ormonde, *Winter's Tale: An Autobiography* (London, 1955)

Index